Your
CAREER
After The
RACE

Helios Herrera

Your Career after the Race

What you can do starting today!

by Helios Herrera

Translated from the original, *Tu carrera después de la carrera*, by Editorial RENUEVO LLC.

ISBN: 978-1-64142-202-4

Published by
Editorial RENUEVO LLC.
www.EditorialRenuevo.com
info@EditorialRenuevo.com

CONTENTS

Dedication

To my three children . . .
and also to you.

"In this book, I want to speak to you the way I hope a perfect stranger will some day talk to my own children when they're your age," Helios.

1940 to 1960

If you don't want your children to starve . . .
go fishing; put food on the table.

1960 to 1980

If you don't want your children to starve . . .
teach them to fish.

1980 to 2000

If you don't want your children to starve . . .
help them buy a fishing pool and give them the best technology available to catch fish.

2000 to 2025

If you don't want your children to starve . . . you must build and operate your own fish farm to make sure there are enough fish.

Acknowledgements

Often, you don't know why someone has appeared in your life; when you open the door, new people and experiences begin entering. That's how this book came to be. I'm grateful to the diverse energies that converged in my life, though from completely different directions, and had such an impact on me . . . before I knew how or why they would.

First, of course, came publicist and media opinion leader Carlos Alazraki, who decided to interview me on his television show and hit me head on in his characteristic style—direct and blunt—asking me straight out: "So what are you doing to help today's youth?," a question that lingered in my mind and found its answer through this book, at the same time that I found a friend for life.

Of course I must mention Max Raphel and Liz Garcia from the UNITEC campus, with whom I began entertaining the creation of a project that would link the experiences of HH Consultores with young adults in our community: "Something good came out of it" after all. Thanks for planting the seed. Later, Felipe Hernandez Tovar, bringing his combined enthusiasm and talent—as a student who at the same time is willing to teach, who at first was only going to contribute a few drawings and ended up running the marathon together with me. Of course, Andres Santillan, who immediately offered his heart and vision, and with whom, I am sure, I will share many more years of awakening and awareness, starting with my own. Thank you, Andres.

They all showed during the same period of my life that lasted less than a year—approaching me from different angles and with completely different life objectives, and of course, were able to align with the other forces already in my life and near to my heart, who also contributed to this book: Fabiola, my wife, a pillar of continuous strength at home, who allowed me to focus on interests beyond our family since I knew that, along the way, she would be in charge of things there. Eleazar Mireles, with his calm presence and gift of projecting that everything is under control. My assistant and helper, Klaudia Nieto, has been a permanent source of support.

I'm grateful to each of them; in one way or another, they've all contributed to the process that led to this book that's goal is to hopefully provide a wonderful launch pad or a catapult for the talent and effort of thousands of young people . . . or even just one.

Thank you, thank you, thank you!

Foreword

If there's one thing all marathon runners agree on, it's this phrase that sums up how we feel each time we cross the finish line: "I'll never do that again!"

A marathon is 26.2-mile race. Does that seem like a walk in the park to you? Well, it's a race that the average person, with a minimum of six months' training, can run in four hours. You must surely know the origin of this fascinating—and at the same time unnatural—sport, but that's not important; what has been truly valuable for me is the training process and discovering how radically I can transform my life thanks to my own effort. That's why I want to share a few analogies between marathon runners and the race of life, hoping that you can appreciate it from a new perspective.

What's unique about accomplishing this feat is that I ran in and trained for marathons while at the same time working professionally in my career, knowing that I was going to come out on top, even if I didn't win first place. This is the first lesson learned for any career.

A marathon is a race, not a team sport; there's no one to blame but yourself if you break down halfway through it. Nor is there anyone else to thank when you reach the finish line. You can train in any kind of terrain, at any time of the year, and wearing any outfit. Running a marathon is an exercise in absolute individual responsibility; your opponent is no one other than yourself and your only objective is to reach the finish line with dignity.

Some think that running a marathon is like D-Day, while others also enjoy training for the race a lot, and view it as just another step necessary for achieving a strong body and spirit, and the culmination of a goal that life gives us at some point or other. It involves many, many, sacrifices. Running is a masochistic exercise with long-term rewards. I think of my marathon training as "the most ungrateful and demanding romantic relationship" of them all. Here's why.

First, your training is like a girlfriend who wants to see you every day giving her the same level of love, support, and attention every time. If you've committed a few sins—she will make you pay. These are the sins you may commit at the taco shop, by staying up all night, by having a few extra drinks or an occasional smoke.

Second, she quickly forgets that you once said you loved her. If you skipped running yesterday, it's like standing your date up— something unforgivable, and your workout will scold you with a cramp in your leg or abdomen or with that terrible feeling of suffocation and nausea during part of your routine.

Third, she couldn't care less about the color you wear, or what you paid for those brand-name sneakers or your watch. What lady race really wants is that you spend a lot of time with her; in her mind, any time you have is quality time. She's very jealous, doesn't want you to play other sports, only to run. She hates soccer or any games that involve a scoreboard, a first and second half, or fans in the bleachers.

Fourth, in order for you to run 26.2 miles, you need to log around 750 miles in 22 to 24 weeks as part of your training. So she only feels she has "proof" that you love her after you've given her your life, soul, and heart. Literally.

As you can see, your precious romantic interest is very demanding. But trust me, the payoff is infinite. This is a transformative, unique, and long-term relationship. It is a metaphor for every step you take in life, every hurdle, and every achievement. It's what you carry inside you and it makes you stronger, more human, and much freer.

I began running marathons at age 22 thanks to my dad's amazing foresight. He, of course, didn't want me to be a professional runner, nor did he want me to bring him my trophies or finalist medals. A father like that would be a selfish parent who only yearns to see his children achieve the successes that he himself didn't accomplish in his own life. What my dad, Felipe Senior, wanted to see was a happy and successful son, despite the setbacks, the adverse terrain, and the temptations along the road. We ran the New York City Marathon together in 1993 and have run many more miles together while training. We learned many things about each other without saying a word, and have cried tears of joy and frustration as we've achieved many milestones by running 10K races every Sunday for many months.

We covered a lot of terrain in our runs on

so many mornings, and in so many different cities and climates, yet were able to surrender ourselves to this journey rather than focusing on the finish line, to enjoy the process of learning with each step what we were capable of doing if we had the will and discipline to keep going.

Over the years, I've never forgotten how to take that first step. And so I've been fortunate enough to run four more marathons. And at the end of each one, I, too, would tell myself: "I'll never do that again!" And I've learned that, although each of us moves at our own pace, we can all go far—very far. There is always a goal awaiting us!

Throughout my dear friend Helios Herrera's book, I will on occasion act as a milepost judge. When the book allows, I'll add my own reflections about running a marathon, which I hope will help your understanding and rouse your interest in the magic of running a race.

I'll see you at the finish line!

Felipe Hernandez Tovar

Chapter ONE

Why do older adults talk to young people as if they're stupid?

I've already been a speaker at 1,500 conferences or seminars—with a cumulative audience equaling more than 2 million people—in the last 22 years of my professional career. I've also taken part in many forums, given many interviews, and shared the stage with hundreds of colleagues.

When the auditorium is filled with young adults, the speaker's tone is almost always the same . . . they talk down to them as if they're stupid.

Older adults are prejudiced; we believe that young people "don't want to take our advice," "they just want to live their lives," and "they aren't willing to adapt to any kind of moral or value structure." And it's likely that these prejudices are well founded.

On the one hand, some of us talk to them as to "children on the way to becoming adults," others project the dilemmas they have with their own children onto them, projecting their fights and traumas, and unconsciously they

21

end up being either more condescending or even harsher.

Why? Why do older adults talk to young people as if they're stupid?

The immediate response that I've gotten from many friends and colleagues is quite clear: "Youths act like fools. They don't pay attention to anyone; they don't seem interested in the real issues; they only think about partying, dating, hanging out and relaxing, and they always look for the fastest way to get things done, the path of least resistance."

I'm sorry to say it, but most of the time my friends are right.

Most young people are absorbed in a kind of social depression, nauseated by false leadership and social confines. Politicians, teachers, businessmen and women, and even religious leaders today say one thing and do another. You see the double standards of your own parents; our society's moral and economic decline is so daunting that who would actually want to get involved with the "big issues"?

The point is that the way young people

behave around each other is one thing; but when they are around adults . . . it's different.

The verdict of hundreds of interviewers seeking to hire new graduates to give them a productive role in life is discouraging:

"They show up late for the interview, without showering. They want to earn a fortune but they don't know how to do anything," and the worst part is that they don't even seem to care how dire their situation is in light of the enormous competition they will face from other candidates.

On the other hand . . . If not when you're young . . . When will there ever be a right time to try dumb things? I would a thousand times rather see an 18-year-old do stupid things than watch a 45-year-old trying to hook up with his daughter's best friend at a party.

How can older adults try to give advice to young people and tell them "how to live" when their own existence leaves much to be desired and is full on drama, double standards, and inconsistencies? If their lives aren't fulfilling, how can adults keep pretending and project what they don't have?

What's your view on this? I also asked a few

young people: why do you act like a fool when an older person speaks to you?

And yes, they're absolutely right; the communication gap between generations is no longer due to a difference in interests; it does have to do with empty morals and a lack of congruence.

However, dear reader, I have bad news for you; this is something that I myself don't like very much:

Due to pure chronological progression, someday you will be the one who finds yourself in the world of young adults and not the adults being the ones who have returned to their youth.

Eventually, you will resist all passion and rebellion trying to disregard your ideals and manners, but if you don't do what is necessary to live up to the requirements of adult life, little by little you will realize that you can't continue to be true to your own ideals and you'll end up trapped in the same mediocrity and incongruence that you so dislike, that you criticize so often, and that separates you so much from the previous generations.

Setting what I've just said aside as a mere

point of reference, I want to make some commitments on my part to you through this book and its possible use in your life, but I'd also like to count on some participation from you.

So, if you allow me, I'm going to suggest what I can offer you in this book and what I expect from you in return; what do you think?

Chapter TWO

Let's make a deal: what to expect from this book

Here's what I'm offering you, and what can you expect from me and from this book:

I promise that I'll never treat you like a fool. I promise to write to you as my equal; I won't go out of my way to "put myself in your shoes at your age so you'll understand me." I won't play the sulking and serious adult trying to act *cool*.

In return, I ask you to give me your word that you won't act like a fool. I want you to promise me that you'll read the whole book, all at once, and to read it with an open mind, investing all the time, space, and energy necessary in order to absorb it.

I'm going to provide you with the data as clearly as possible; I won't try to manipulate you into taking any particular action. It's not my intent to make you feel good or bad or any particular way, nor will I try to "motivate you" or "cheer you on." That's not why I'm here. I just want to provide objective information, numbers, and a description of the reality that awaits you.

In return, I ask that before rejecting this

information outright by deciding that I'm talking about something too far in the future, you'll give me the benefit of the doubt, and have a little faith in my intentions to contribute to your development process. Think of me as a friend along the road, and I give you my word of honor that the information you'll read in these next pages will be useful to you in the years to come. Think of my advice like the condom you carry in your wallet or purse—you may not need it at this exact moment, but when you do need it . . . it's a good thing to have at hand.

I promise that:

. . . without being flippant, I'll try to be as lighthearted as possible, and will try my best to make my writing easy to read . . .

More than just something to read, I want this book to open up a channel of communication between us that will allow us, if you want, to have a conversation. I want you to feel that you're having a conversation with me rather than reading something I've written.

In return, I ask you to let down your guard, to relax so we can enjoy our time together, that if you don't agree with me about something, you'll let me know openly by sending me an email—but not limit yourself to only sending negative feedback, and instead provide me with productive input about what you disagree with and why.

I promise:

. . . to personally answer each and every email you send me. I receive many and sometimes it takes me a few days to respond, but I answer them all. Now, thanks to the wonders of social media, I can share my answer to the same question with many people at the same time. You can reach me at helios@hhconsultores.com and on other social media. You'll find my other contact info at the end of this book.

In return, I ask that you:

1. Sign up for my virtual newsletter, I'll send you at least one article of general interest every month: www.hhconsultores.com .

2. Communicate clearly and objectively; be clear and precise when you send me a message.

3. If you're looking for a specific kind of answer, let me know so that I can provide it.

4. If I've already answered the same question,

suggestion, or comment that you have on my blog or webpage, please don't email it to me.

5. Actively and enthusiastically participate in the community blog and on my website.

And last but not least:

I promise to be as honest and direct as possible, I'm not suggesting that you "like" me or give me a "thumbs down." Nor am I looking for any response at all; I'm only here to help and make suggestions.

If at the end of this "adventure," it turns out that we also "hit it off," fantastic; we'll join each other's social networks, but if not . . . we can part on friendly terms, as if we never met and are as anonymous as ever—pressing delete is all it will take for you to get rid of me.

In return, I ask you to make a daily, conscientious effort to make your life one that's worth living.

Chapter THREE

Sensitizing Yourself

Why your mouth starts hurting before they've pulled the tooth

"None so deaf as those who will not hear and none so blind as those who will not see."

In the 1980s, the most powerful and lethal epidemic up to that point in the modern era was happening: AIDS.

It turned out that the era of sexual openness—which was perhaps the last frontier of human freedom and expression in freedom according to those who lived through the times of "peace and love"—was already over; from now on; it would be necessary to follow rules, rituals, and protocols with sex too. The issue was, and still is, much more of a cultural problem than a medical one—that people said: "I won't get it," "There's no way I'll get infected." To this day, there are still millions of carriers who don't dare to get tested, mainly . . . for fear of testing positive. What nonsense! Don't you think? As if ignoring the problem solves anything. But for asinine people with small brains, it seems that "Ignorance is bliss" is their motto, along with "if I don't know I have problem, I don't need to do anything to solve it."

Of course, part of this book's purpose is precisely this, to raise your awareness—

well actually to help you become sensitive to certain situations—but let's not confuse raising your awareness about something with becoming sensitive to it, because these are two different things.

In the previous passage I told you that AIDS was a social problem, and today mainly one of ignorance, apathy or stupidity. I know you're even nodding your head and thinking,"Hey, this dude's right, problems don't get solved on their own," so you're aware of the situation. So then. . . when was the last time you had an AIDS test?

Being conscious is not always enough to make us take action; information isn't very useful by itself because it only affects the cognitive part of our brain. A process takes place between understanding and acting, which I refer to as "to take ownership" of the information by creating behaviors and actions to go with it.

In order to take ownership, we need both information and an emotional connection, or as Alberto Cortez sings:

Because what we love

we consider our own property.

And he's right—when we add emotion to a concept, it becomes ours. Awareness through sensitivity, then, attempts to make you feel "something," confronting the raw information head on, but from the angle that allows you to look at yourself in the mirror and challenge yourself . . .

"And what the heck do I do when faced with this reality and all this? Why does it matter to me?"

If we were sensitive and aware, we wouldn't need to increase our awareness of what's happening on the outside; the point is that we are all sensitive and aware, but we are gradually desensitizing ourselves. Let me give an example:

Feeling pain in our body is a stoplight, a message from our nervous system that alerts our brain that "something is wrong here," and then the brain responds by sending the sensation of pain to that specific area to make us take appropriate action by withdrawing from the source of the pain.

That's why when you lift a hot container off the stove, within milliseconds your nerve endings send your brain information about the high temperatures you sensed when you touched the container, and also within milliseconds the sensation of pain returns to your hand and you pull it away from the surface.

So that our environment adapts to our needs, humans have designed instruments, technologies, and devices to desensitize us or protect us from pain, ranging from a special cloth to handle hot containers to oven mitts; the idea is to be able to handle the container (and live) despite its high temperature and to be able to use it.

When a tooth starts hurting, it's a sure sign that "something's wrong in there." What do we do then? Do we go to the dentist? Usually not right away, the easiest thing is to take medication that eases the pain; and so we manage to fix the symptoms of our problems, but do little about what's causing them. What "was wrong in there" no longer hurts, but the issue surely hasn't been fixed and is possibly getting worse. By the time you're brave enough to go to the dentist, what could have been solved with a simple filling ends involving an extraction or an even bigger procedure.

Turning to palliatives and painkillers is as absurd as trying to correct an error on a page you've just printed; instead of opening the file and correcting the word where it was first entered or misspelled. We turn into perpetual proofreaders, yet the printer keeps producing the same mistake on the page every time. Then you blame the printer.

So I'm going to give you some clear, comprehensive advice by way of warning, but never as a threat—I not only want to make you aware, but to sensitize you.

Warnings are merely a signal that you're exposing yourself to danger, whether or not you actually do it; whether you actually do it or not, threat is the promise that you will hurt yourself if you do.

Of course, everyone reads what they want to in the warning; they may see the signal of danger in their path, but it will be decoded, given meaning, or owned (remember that term?) by your brain. So it's possible that you'll hear what you want to hear when you're given a warning, and understand or interpret it in a way that lets you evade reality, as in the example of someone who doesn't get tested for AIDS for fear of finding out and confirming that they are positive, while someone else picks up the hot container with the help of a heat-resistant cloth.

One of the scenes that most influenced my career 20 years ago was in *Discovering the Future*, a film produced by paradigm expert, futurologist, and consultant Dr. Joel Barker produced in 1989.

I'll try to describe what happens:

In the movie, a young man is driving at high speed on a dirt road in a small town; adrenaline explodes in his body and makes him accelerate as he goes faster and faster. Suddenly, as he is rounding a sharp curve, an oncoming old truck driven by an older woman suddenly appears. The young man manages to swerve and avoid hitting her, but clearly hears her yell: "Pig!" at him, to which he almost instinctively replies: "Stupid Cow!" his voice filled with emotion and anger. The young man floors the accelerator again, now furious. "You old hag! What's wrong with you? If you call me names, I'm going to insult you right back." All these thoughts were racing through his mind when, taking the next curve at full speed—

He collides with a pig!

Well, of course the lady tried to warn him, but the young man felt threatened, his belief systems and emotions connected to the information prevented him from realizing that she was really trying to tell him.

Many people who are close to you have tried to "warn you" about things, too; however, the interpretation we give to their warnings makes them sound like "threats" to us. Even if these concepts overlap, they differ on an emotional level.

"If you don't do x, then y is going to happen to you" is a statement that can be read as a threat or as a warning, no matter how it was said or written. So you are going to run into a lot of "pigs" in the future. My intention is simply to tell you where you're likely to find them on the road, and beyond what curves you'll find even more, so that you'll be more careful out there and fine-tune your navigating skills.

What I'm trying to say is that some situations

will be painful enough that you go to the dentist before the tooth is full of cavities, but not so painful that they overwhelm you to the point of thinking that you believe you can't do anything about it and don't feel like moving at all; in fact, the opposite is true.

This is the best time in your life to read this book

I started my career as a marathon runner one Sunday at 7:30 in the morning. I had a hangover from bingeing with my college friends the night before. Then my dad showed up at my door with a pair of tennis shoes in hand and, instead of asking me what time I'd gotten home or how many drinks I'd had, he said, "Do you want to go to New York?"

Chapter FOUR

You'll make the most important
decisions of your life when you
have the least experience

Tu carrera después de la carrera

Life happens backwards. Imagine a utopia that goes like this: we are born at age 85, full of wisdom, knowledge and experience—knowing in advance what life is and where to look as we go down the road and enjoy the landscape, knowing what will really be the things we remember, what we enjoy, what is worth the trouble and what isn't.

If this were the case, then our childhoods would be much safer; from age 85 to 74, the slowness of our movements would help us avoid accidents and unnecessary accelerations, and every day we would be open to the experience of knowing that we can move more and better.

Our adolescence . . . around age 72, would be tremendously easy to deal with! Just imagine! Who at that age would give a heck about having pimples on their face? Our sexuality would just be awakening as the symptoms of menopause and andropause began. Well, we would take it all more calmly, we wouldn't get anyone pregnant or get pregnant, that is, the experimentation would be a little less stressful, we would need to apply more quality than quantity to the process, and from here we would move into adulthood.

At the beginning of our productive phase, we would bring all our accumulated life experience with us; we would be productive from the start and make the most of our time; we would do business and consolidate our career without mistakes and losses. Our marriages would also be richer by bringing together two people who are fully present and able to more fully enjoy each other. We would enter our third age with money, our health, and experience and knowledge. If we had the money and time to travel, we wouldn't make ourselves look ridiculous by buying sports cars. Finally, we would spend our last 5 years enjoying childhood cleanly, preparing our souls, and going before the Creator in all our purity, after having enjoyed human experience to the fullest.

It would be so amazing . . . but that's not the way it is

I'm very excited to create this material with young people in mind. You should know that between the ages of 17 and 25, you'll be making the most important decisions of your life—those that will impact the rest of it, for better or for worse. What should you study? Who will you marry? Will you have children and if so, how many? What bad habits from youth will you carry with you for the next 20 years? What do you end up getting into and where? How do you mess up, what do you smoke, what kind of music do I listen to? What are you going to do in life? Where do you want to live in? Etc., etc.

Based on the decisions you make now, and with the passage of time, life will begin to fill you up with its conditions and obligations. The empty, lightweight backpack that allows you freedom and mobility now begins to fill with burdens and responsibilities. Very soon, all decisions begin to be made from the standpoint of: "what do I need or what can I do?" instead of: "what do I want my life to be like?"

That's why it's so exciting to talk to you now, as you are beginning to build your life, and not when you're 40, have already started the race, and want to add an additional story to the foundation of your life.

Unfortunately, the decisions that will most impact your future are made at a time when you've had the fewest experiences. We lose control over what we want to happen in our lives and how it should happen simply because of our lack of knowledge, and since we don't want to learn our lesson from anyone else or to live a life too much like those of the adults, we just don't pay a lot of attention to their advice at all.

"If they really had something to teach me, they wouldn't have ended up like they are," right?

So okay, please try not to be too hard on the adults around you; what they have to tell you on many occasions is not advice on "how you should do it," but about "how they did it and how it went." They are trying to explain how they would do it themselves if they could start over again. Yes, you're right, nothing guarantees that if they tried again now and did something differently, they would do it any better; that is, they're trying to communicate the experience they had, instead of passing on the knowledge they accumulated. Of course, your perceptions, judgment, and analysis are keen:

What can I really know about you based on your answers? And as if that weren't enough, due to an imbalance in our society, we are used to seeing much more bad than good, so the outcomes we use to judge adults who want to have a say in our life and in our future are usually not what we want to achieve.

I'm going let you in on a secret . . . you'll never find a leader congruent enough to live up fully to your expectations or to look to as a model; if you find such a person, be careful to follow them with your head and not your heart, because this may be a professional manipulator.

Getting advice is like buying tomatoes at a farmers' market. From many to choose from, pick the ones that you think are right for you, and above all, decide when you want to eat them. If within three days, they should be a little harder and less ripe, but don't buy them from the farmer's advice.

You can choose to live a life worth peanuts, but life can also be an extraordinary experience

Let me say this plainly and objectively: You don't belong to your parents, you don't belong to your partner or your children, and just in case you really believe this one, you'd barely even belong to God, but beyond religion and mysticism, you truly only belong to yourself. Your only obligations are to yourself, and here is the only real commitment you have regarding what you are going to do with your life and who you are going to be in life. Therefore, you can make your life exactly what you want it to be; it will be you and only you who will live it, for better or for worse.

When you rebel against an authority figure and shout: "Don't mess with my life!" You are absolutely right, especially if that authority figure tries invasively and with impunity to control you, ignore your choices, or decide the course of your destiny and your future for you.

But be careful . . . I don't know a single parent who makes the worst mistake imaginable hoping to hurt their children. It's possible that what you take to be an invasion of your autonomy is truly a genuine effort to help you find the best path, at least in the eyes of those who try, to guide you based on their own experiences and to help you not make the same mistakes that they did or even new mistakes of your own.

At the end of the day, you write your life story through your decisions; and the best or only real advice I can offer you is that you make most of them as fully aware as possible of the risks and with an understanding that you accept your actions and consequences.

When you turn right instead of going left, the thing of least consequence is the impact of the decision; what you are really deciding is "where you're going and how to get there."

All your decisions involve both a "here

and now" and a "there and later." You make most of your choices in the "here and now," even though their consequences will reach into the "there and later." How often you make decisions now sends ripples into the future exponentially, that is, every time you take action today, you multiply all the possible repercussions of their consequences.

Let me give an example: if you decide to eat a poor diet today, you'll have health problems tomorrow, or at least, you'll multiply and increase the chances that you will in the future. If you make the choice to eat like this every day, you multiply your odds of future obesity. Perhaps eating poorly for "just once a week" isn't as serious as making this a "six-day-a-week" habit.

If you decide to have unprotected sex "here and now," you'll either wind up with a sexually transmitted illness or with pregnancies "there and later," or at least increase the odds that those consequences will happen. The premise is the same . . . doing it "once without protection" increases the possibility less than doing it "six times without protection," but in this case, just one of those six errors in judgment is all it takes to have unintended consequences. You are simply increasing the odds.

At the same time, if you decide to work hard and focus on "here and now," you will have success and stability "there and later." This isn't certain either, but multiply the possibilities that things will turn out in your favor.

You can choose to live a life worth peanuts, but finding the pearls it contains can be an extraordinary experience; remember what Peter Drucker said:

"The best way to predict the future . . . is to create it."

As a final consideration before getting into the tough stuff, I must say a few words about resilience.

Chapter FIVE

Resilience: it doesn't matter where you came from; what's important is where you're going

Running is one of the world's cheapest sporting activities, and at the same time is capable of creating one of the biggest payoffs and pleasures that a human can experience. It doesn't require investing in special equipment. I started running in some used sneakers that I bought one day during one of the many attempts to exercise. The only thing I knew was that they fit me and that they would help me to take the first step, so I took the leap. What was the worst that could happen? I never even thought about it.

In science, "resilience" is the ability of matter to spring back to its original state or shape. So when you stretch a rubber band and then release it, resilience is what allows it to spring back to its original shape.

Why am I telling you this? Because it's possible that we can all visualize where we are going and what we want from life, and in that sense, the advice is the same for everyone:

"Research and find out what you need to do in order to do what you want to do . . . and then do it, " but the starting point is not the same for everyone.

Some are born just a few feet from the starting line; others are born a little further away from it, that's all. We can't pretend that the chances of achieving success are the same for those on the starting line as for those waiting to start the race from a mile and a half behind it.

But we mustn't assume that those who finish last or in the middle of the pack can't also successfully reach their goals, and sometimes even place first.

The race in question doesn't only reward the winner; it really is a race against your own best time. In the end, everyone who makes it will be rewarded; it's merely a question of "where did you place this time and how far did you move up on the qualifying list?".

Clearly and bluntly, I must tell you that your origin isn't nearly as important as your destination.

Despite all the information that you will read in the next sections, or better still, along with it,

the outcome of your life and your career isn't
determined by statistics; there is no such thing
as divine destiny. Your future will be equal to
the sum of your decisions and the actions that
define it.

If you have been unlucky enough to start the
race from further behind, if life hasn't given you
the same opportunities as daddy's boy, the guy
with all the money, surely it's given you other
advantages. If you didn't grow up being served
on a silver platter, but you had to learn to make
it or put food on the table yourself, surely the
process of development that you went through
to do so provided you with other kinds of
experiences; therefore, you will have access to a
different group of people and you will be more
empowered than others to solve certain types
of problems.

Your resilience will allow you to "spring back
to your original shape." When you were born,
when you came into the world, you were neither
more nor less than anybody else's child; you
come from the same essence.

You made no apologies for yourself,
and didn't know about excuses or negative
mindsets, nor did you know about awards

and incentives, outside stimuli or any other social groups.

If you started the race from "further back," it will probably be more difficult, but in the end you can either choose to run even further than those at the starting line, or use your life story as an excuse to never even start. Once again, the consequences will depend on the decisions you intentionally make—here and now.

When you drive a car, that little mirror in front of you, above the dash, the rearview mirror, allows you to remember where you came from, but you must focus your attention on where you're going . . . very soon, you'll even start to see that your starting point seems to be lost in

Without realizing it, I was in the middle of the forest where it was only 35° F degrees and I was running in the dark. I only heard my own footsteps and my breathing. I'd been awake for half an hour and didn't even remember how I'd gotten there. But I was sure that I was going somewhere and that my only companion was my will to do it. The race had started and there was no going back.

the background as you choose to continuing

moving forward. What you see through the rearview mirror will provide a systematic update of what you've been achieving, of how far you've come.

Chapter SIX

Your career . . . it really is a race

As soon as I finish up the last required credits, I'll slightly revise my thesis or end up going for an automatic degree option."

And now what?

It seems completely out of sync with reality, but unfortunately there are still thousands of young people who believe that the race ends as soon as they show the diploma to their parents.

And the fact is that there are so many youths who waste their time in the classroom! You spend more than five years going to college, even when you know in advance that the reason you're there is only a formality because you have something completely different in mind for your career, and the only reason you're going is to be able to hand your parents the document that they've "waited so long for," either because of their own traumas and issues or because they believe, as we've already established, that they are doing "the best for you" by pushing you to finish your university education.

If this is your situation, I really have little to say to you—unless you are really willing to take a look at the real race. Not only are you not prepared for it, but you've also lost valuable time, and as a result, are already lagging behind in your place at the starting line . . .

. . . in this fast-paced, globalized world.

"Not advancing is going backwards."

Other people believe that university education is a form of safe-conduct, a first-class boarding pass that guarantees you a place on the stage with the successful podium finishers . . . Sadly I must inform you, my dear friend, that there is no such thing as a guarantee. The only thing you know you have for sure when you hold a college degree in your hands . . . is that you have a college degree.

Let's be clear about this and look at it with the blunt honesty and objectivity that the topic requires: when, after almost 18 continuous years of study (6 in elementary school, 2 in secondary school, 4 in high school, and at least 4 more from undergraduate, if not 2 additional years for a Master's degree), you can finally wear the gown and throw the cap to the sky, you feel proud and happy because you've finished your degree.

But sadly, you've actually only finished your training for the marathon! The real race and competition have only just begun

During the race there will be no teachers to correct your mistakes or give you reports; there will be self-conscious bosses with egos who will transfer their own trauma onto you. There will be no honor rolls or "extraordinary achievement" awards; there will be promotions or firings and layoffs. You will not be able to "skip classes." If you skip work, you'll face the hardship of unemployment or, as I like to say, underemployment. Very few people will care one iota what you really know or don't know, or whether or not you are actually ready to practice your profession—you'll simply be judged by the objective measure of your tangible results.

I don't want to dismiss the value of a university education—that's the furthest thing from my mind; but I do want to look at it objectively.

Imagine the starting line of the New York Marathon; around 80,000 people sign up every year, of them, more than 30,000 are rejected before they even start the race! That means, on the big day 50,000 runners leave the starting line—all running at the same time, but with different goals in mind. Some have a genuine interest in winning the marathon; others, most in fact, will settle for finishing it under their own best time, and at least a few others will celebrate with their friends just for having participated in a marathon at all, without caring too much where they rank on the list, and even if they didn't finish the race.

NYC Marathon, 2008. Greenbox

Using this analogy, do you really think that people who start a marathon in 3,000th or 3,500th place behind everyone else have any possible chance of coming in first? It's a physically impossible question. The number of competitors in front of them would create a lag time of at least 20 minutes between those who started out in the lead and the time it takes everyone else to get to the line after working through the crowd of runners at the starting line and beginning the race. That is, if your goal is to win the competition, you are simply out of the running. On the other hand, if your goal is to run the marathon, finish it, and improve your time, you still have a chance as long as you clock your time from the moment you cross the starting line, and not from when the official fired the starting pistol and everyone was off.

NYC Marathon, 2008.
Greenbox

Therefore, having a university education, of course, adds value to your life from the beginning, it puts you on the track and enters you in the race! Those who simply don't have it can't "register for the New York World Championship," or are among the first 30,000 to be rejected; they must stay home in their cities and settle for competing in minor races. They will still be able to run the 10K sponsored by a local company in town where, of course, the prize pool for winners is simply nonexistent.

This is more or less how life is.

When you finish the training stage in life, your career as a race begins with a course that begins with plain and simple survival, to rise to the top of corporate, economic, social, and spiritual success . . . What is your personal goal? Do you want to win the race and take the prize bag or trophy home? Do you want to just run and improve your stamina and ranking year after year, gradually working toward an upward professional career trajectory? Is it enough for you just to run it? What is your personal expectation for your career?

You can certainly tell me something like: "Helios, I have no idea what my goal is for that race!" "I'll worry about my goal when that day comes," or "How do you expect me to focus on something that's so far, far away in the future?" (Read this with sarcasm).

Well, to keep my promise I'm only going to give you the information . . .

You know what information you need, and what you'll discard, but the purpose is to tell you—in the most logical terms possible—about possible strategies you should start to consider in your training and that they will vary depending on your goals.

Anyone can understand that a long-distance marathon runner must prepare their body for a race that's much longer than 26 miles, and eats, exercises, and prepares for that specific feat, while in the case of another high-performance athlete, a 100-meter dash runner, you also consume 500% more carbohydrates a day and build muscle mass three times faster than normal.

The athlete in question does not think: "I'm a runner, I'm training to race . . . I could compete in the Olympics either by running a marathon or in the 100-meter dash" if they selected me or "I'm going to register for all the event categories . . . let's see what I can do!".

The only way to enhance the knowledge acquired during your professional training in college is for you to have a more or less clear idea about what objectives you'll be pursuing as your focus from now on. You can't start worrying when you cross that bridge. You must be concerned about it starting today.

The enormous amount of mediocrity that exists in our Latinx societies is due to a large extent on this attitude; while individuals who grow up in the major world powers begin developing their competencies and skills from childhood, clarifying and planning 25 years in advance. Economic conditions in most third-world countries don't allow for so much vision; with this cultural outlook, we must solve problems immediately; then, we learned to live, plan, and prepare for a competition that's happening at the end of next month . . .not to compete for the rest of our lives.

How many of your friends at school only study to pass the exam?

Just think about it: you either erase information or keep it organized in your short-term memory; once you've taken an exam, you replace that information with what you need to know for the next test, a new subject, the next credits you'll need to graduate. At the end of the day, the knowledge you should have retained ends up forgotten . . . and in the best-case scenario remains in the bibliographical sources where you first found it. So in conclusion: you finish your training, you graduate, and you face a job market that requires you to know how to "do something" with what you've learned, not just to have memorized data.

"What I learned in school has nothing to do with real life," is a phase I often hear.

But let's not point the blame only at educational systems and institutions. If you weren't linking the new knowledge you were supposed to be attaining with a future goal, the techniques and theories were both lost in time and in your memory.

Therefore, I want to invite you to come up with a clear idea of the type of athlete you intend to become and to decide what categories you want to compete in, so that from now on you can choose to train using the best and most systematic strengthening routine to work the appropriate "muscles" for the necessary length required to help prepare you.

Cramming the night before an exam is crazy

If I read, understand, and answer all the questionnaires and self-evaluations in the modern manual for learning to swim, will I be able to swim? Will my body know what to do and how to do it? Of course not! A combination of attitude, knowledge, and action are the three ingredients that must be brought together dynamically over time.

The development of a skill is not only a collection of data and theoretical knowledge; it is also about taking ownership of those knowledge and skills . . . time and anticipation. Say it takes two people nine months to create a baby; if you want to speed up the process, you can't bring nine couples together and expect the baby to be born in only a month.

Returning to the subject of a college education, let me emphasize that I'm not underrating it. Taking courses, finishing college, and earning a bachelor's degree is very important, even more so in the competitive world that we live in today. In fact, I remember that in my generation our training, let's say officially, ended with a bachelor's degree; few, very few ventured on to get a master's degree, which at the time was a prestigious and impressive degree to have finished. Not to mention a doctorate degree—going that far was truly aspirational, almost idealized by the general population. Meeting a "doctor of architecture" was almost like saying that one of your in-laws is related to Indiana Jones (a character who also existed at that time—

mentioning him means that I was definitely young in the 80s). Things are very different now; your formal university training ends with your first graduate degree. Let's say that, if you aspire to be a marathon runner, they won't even sell you the registration form if you have less than a master's degree. And so, from the get-go, corporate success is becoming increasingly elitist. If you add globalization to that, it really puts us at a disadvantage, not because of capacity, but because of our cultural attitude.

While China (the world's most populous country) trains its citizens since childhood with clarity about what they want and how they want it to be, and adjust their mental structure to achieve it from the time they are young, we continue to think that "when the time comes, I'll start thinking about it." If we recognize that global competitiveness is increasing due to a logical formula of supply and demand, then we must also understand and recognize what our efforts during the training and preparation stage should be, if not more emphatic, then certainly more focused.

Already, a bachelor's degree isn't enough of a "credential" to register for the New York

Marathon and stand in the section with the first 5,000 competitors by the starting line—that area is restricted only to those who have already completed two postgraduate degrees and have eight years of successful experience. If you aspire to start from a good vantage point near the beginning of the course, you must define your goal at the beginning of your university preparation, start working now and literally "worrying" about the future, start doing something before you need to, and you will have those skills when you need them.

I'm sure that your generation includes friends and classmates who study and work, and you'll notice that their focus, objectivity, and the approach they take to their university education is different.

On the one hand, they may need to qualify to be eligible for a promotion in their job, which of course entails a different set of economic opportunities. You'll also notice that they have very little time to waste, that they're not happy when an instructor cancels class, and that they're against university strikes and walkouts that result in wasted time. Surely you know a classmate who, in addition to studying and working, has to run after class to pick up their child from kindergarten and deals with a spectacular level of daily stress.

In keeping with my original promise, I'm not going to treat you like you're stupid. I know perfectly well that you understand your classmate or colleague's situation, and I also know you think you have everything under control. Part of being young is thinking—or wanting to believe—that you are indestructible, that you have unlimited energy, or that you would never be stupid enough to let something like that to even happen to you. But let me share some more information with you . . .

It's very likely that today before leaving home you will have gone to the refrigerator and found that "someone" put "something" there; what's more, it may be that that this "something" has not even been to your total liking, and that you've complained to that "someone" . . . "Dang it, *someone*! Don't you know that this 'something' is not the 'something' that I like?!" Still, you've probably taken some of that "something" and swallowed it reluctantly, but you managed to eat before leaving home.

That same "someone" pays for the electricity, the telephone, the rent or the mortgage, clothes and vacations, and possibly your school tuition, as well as your books and lab fees, well, that "someone" supports your needs and, although sometimes you think they don't do a very good job of it, rest assured that they are giving it their best effort.

Of course here you could yell: "You know what, Helios . . .? I didn't ask to be born; they brought me into this world so they can take care of me, and that's that. The one who invites someone pays the bill, and now they need to pay up."

And that's fine, I'm not going to press the point any further and leave the matter there; but first, once again let me give you some information.

You're lucky to have both parents. Hundreds of fathers leave their children and their children's mothers; there are now increasingly more single mothers raising children than children growing up in stable marriages, and also hundreds of single mothers who are simply unable to provide the minimum necessary to a child until he or she reaches college age. Remember and appreciate that, despite all the possible shortcomings you experienced growing up or the things you lacked, despite you can't wear a new pair of the latest brand name tennis shoes every 8 weeks, you're really lucky that "someone" put "food on the table."

But taking this gift for granted (which is not so good) . . . if you admit that you're lucky and if I in turn agree that "they" "must" keep you fed—then case closed?

Now that we've put an end to a fruitless discussion, I'll continue. You probably have hopes and dreams today; you can visualize your destiny with optimism and enthusiasm, you know that you have the support of that "someone" and that they will do everything in their power to offer you a sustainable reality and a promising future.

But I'm going to predict something for you: in a very short time, and almost without you realizing it, you will be the one who must play the role of that "someone" and put "something" in the fridge for someone else.

Almost without realizing what's happened, you're going to fall in love and, one way or another, you'll start your own family or else wind up being someone's caregiver; I guarantee that you are going to have a partner and probably children before—long before the fruits of your university training will be reflected in your pocketbook. More than 50% of university dropouts leave precisely due to the impossibility of sustaining the economic rhythm and schedule that maintaining a family requires while studying at the same time. Again, you only have to look at the reality of your peers to verify these statistics. How many started? How many are still going? How many do you think will finish? How many will really have the possibility of transcending their current existence and practicing their profession while making a difference in the world? How many remain trapped living paycheck-to-paycheck while making sure that their family survives? But the most important thing is:

Where will you be as far as all those "how many" questions?

If you had to take on financial responsibility for supporting your household today, do you know how much money it takes to continue living as you've been living? Do you have any idea what you would need to do—and how you would do it—to provide that amount? Are you aware that even if you're invincible and indestructible, your parents may not be? The main reason a talented young person fails to develop to their full potential and become *young talent* is because life caught up with them before they expected it to in some way or other.

In the next chapter, I'm going to share with you some numbers and statistics about what happens to young people who are considered talented, but I want you to know beforehand that the main reason why a talented young person does *not* achieve their full potential is because life interferes with their dreams before they are ready. For whatever reason, they are forced to veer away from their dreams and career to focus instead on supporting themselves financially and end up stumbling through today's tough economy.

So their talent remains like an uncut gemstone, a raw material that they can never transform into something else. Their situation becomes a bit like the canvas and oil paints you once bought, promising to paint a beautiful picture, but that are still waiting in the back of the closet because you never had time to use them, because other priorities that needed your attention came first. As the years go by, your schedule becomes tighter and tighter, your commitments grow, any windows of free time you had narrow; paradoxically, the potential talent you had that could have really helped you through these daily problems never had a chance to develop, to the point that you are confused by it and then lose it through the stress of your daily routine.

When is the life I want going to begin?

The main reason a talented person fails to develop their full potential and become a Young Talent is because life somehow catches up with them before they are ready.

There came a time when I no longer wanted to be a runner; I didn't want to sacrifice my weekends and my friends, or miss out on all the fun other guys my age were having. I didn't like falling asleep at the movies or not wanting to go for a walk with my girlfriend because my legs hurt. But my dream of getting across that finish line was becoming more and more of an obsession for me.

Chapter SEVEN

A "Young Talent" is someone who . . .

What I discovered after reading and analyzing presentations and discussions facilitated by the OECD in 2009, a «Young Talent» is someone who—having finished their university training (and statistically with a master's degree)—is able to practice their profession while earning enough to continuously improve their standard of living thanks to it.

To clarify, a "Young Talent" is someone who earns enough through their career to change their lifestyle and standard of living—economically, as well as both culturally and socially.

With my characteristic pragmatism and being overly simplistic here, let me put this into the simplest terms: *If your family was bringing in 20 dollars a day in income before you graduated, you should have the ability to make at least 21 dollars following your degree once you begin working in that field.* In your social sphere, you should be able to positively impact your environment thanks to practicing your profession; culturally, having that training and education gives you a beyond-average range of knowledge, artistic appreciation and enjoyment of both your peers and your predecessors.

If you take into consideration that, even after completing their bachelors' degrees, more than 70% of university graduates still accept low-paying jobs, starting out almost like an apprentice or trainee and earning a paycheck that's less than the monthly cost of their tuition, their parents' salaries, or what the government paid the institution where they studied, we can at least in part predict, based on the statistics, how difficult your situation is likely to be and what your chances are of becoming a "Young Talent." I don't mean that you aren't already a talented young person, since the adjective "talented" indicates that you possess many talents; I'm referring to the term "Young Talent" in a completely practical and pragmatic sense.

I remember seeing a ton of cars the first time I was in a National University of Mexico (UNAM) parking garage.

Most were older models, or at least three or four years old, sometimes there was a newer model, and a few makes and models that are considered status symbols.

One might think that the most expensive and luxurious cars would belong to the professors, or to professionals who have made their way after years studying and expanding in their specialty, or to those experts in their field who can recite a continuous steam of the data, techniques, and theories regarding their subject of study. The sad truth is that most professors often either didn't own a car, or their cars are very modest, and even though they use the existential excuse: "I have the car so that I can get from point A to point B; I don't need anything bigger or better than this." Still, we all knew that if they could afford it, they would have upgraded to a better model. Most of the cars that you see on campus belong to the students, especially those who come from well-to-do families. Once in a while, the student driving is a young man or woman who indeed works and studies, who for years has maintained a modest income, and whose savings allowed them, through perseverance and discipline, the luxury of buying a nice car.

And, the plain and simple truth is: people don't get paid for what they know, but for what they are able to do with what they know.

Therefore, people with a low level of knowledge but a high level of skill in putting what they do know into practice will be able to position themselves much better in the working world than those "walking encyclopedias" who don't have the ability to transfer their knowledge into the real-world job market.

But I've gotten off track. We were talking about what it means to be "Young Talent."

Of course, at your age, the world is too small for you. If, at a moment when I'm filled with overflowing enthusiasm, I asked your entire group of peers in the middle of the auditorium . . . "who here is going to become a future "Young Talent"? The resounding response—somewhere between euphoria, a rush of endorphins, and mockery—would be "me!" This reaction indicates your optimism, positive attitude, and the confidence you have in yourself. Some of your peers might simply feel too confident and unmotivated to even bother raising their hands or answer the question, saying to themselves: "This guy is a complete clown . . . I'm already a 'Young Talent;' I don't have to prove it; I don't even need to answer his idiotic question. I'm not even going to give him the time of day or because his question doesn't deserve an answer."

But dear readers! The bad news is that this

question of being a "Young Talent" doesn't have much to do with you at all or your desire to be one, or with your attitudes or stance when I ask the question. The matter in question is emphatically, pragmatically, objectively, and completely based on statistics and data—believe what you believe, and feel whatever you feel about it. At the end of the day, the question is a basic one; it doesn't even matter what your grade point average is nor the number of test waivers you're approved; this issue of "talent" has much more to do with your ability to put what you've learned into practice and to produce tangible results in your social, cultural, and work environments.

People don't earn money because of what they know, but because of what they can do with what they know

From a vocational point of view, the job you've trained for—that is, your profession—should be enough to completely satisfy your economic and emotional needs.

You should not only be able to provide for yourself and your family through the sufficient, constant, and stable source of income you bring home by working in your field; your work must also be fulfilling for you. It should allow you the sublime experience of personal growth through the gradual accumulation of experiences and the challenges you achieve. It is by working as a professional, at least in the ideal of life, that you'll find the integrity to keep both your needs and your family's needs satisfied. (I'm talking about the family that you will create as a father or mother, not the one that you are part of today as a son or daughter).

> *After two or three 10K races under my belt, I became a fan of running shirts, designer shoes, sunglasses, and timepieces. I started spending the monthly allowance my dad gave me on registration fees for races, bus tickets so I could travel and run on the beach, sports drinks, socks, magazines with running advice, a music player.*
>
> *Because there wasn't enough money for everything, I set to work writing articles about my experiences of running. Some friends and I started publishing a journal every two weeks with observations, photos, and the anecdotes from other crazy runners who, like me, also wanted to take racing seriously. Advertisers became interested, and I started my first business.*

Chapter EIGHT

Practicing your profession should generate wealth

I don't want to only focus on money in this book, nor to suggest that your profession should satisfy only your financial needs; but being 100% realistic here, if your profession doesn't allow you to live and live well economically, it will hardly be able to support your more spectacular and bigger dreams.

If your profession fills your soul, but not your bank account, then you're doing "something" wrong, since any job, any professional performance when well done, must have an economic value in the setting in which you performed it.

Carlos Islas, who was at that time the president of AXA University, told me in an interview I did with him, that "money is work encapsulated." So your work, the results or products you give to your employer or client, will have a cost and a value. Economic, spiritual, and family wealth—or wealth of any kind, is obtained though problem-solving. If you want to earn money, solve a problem; if you want to earn more money . . . solve more problems.

A scene from Pedro Infante's and Luis Aguilar's entertaining film *Full Speed Ahead* comes to mind, where a neighborhood superintendent, wearing a certain type of work uniform, comes running out of his house and shouts to his wife, "I'm off, *Vieja!*" as he goes to work; hours later he bursts back into the scene saying, "I'm back, *Vieja*," only to reappear at the door barely 30 seconds later wearing a different work uniform and saying "I'm off, *Vieja!*".

Do you want more money? Then find more problems to fix. Of course there are only 24 hours in a day, so no matter how enthusiastic and positive you may be, there will come a moment when you don't have time to work a second or third job . . . . Do you still want to earn more? Well then look for more expensive problems to fix that will also bring in larger monetary winnings.

This is the foundation of a vocational training—equipping yourself with knowledge, techniques, and concepts that will allow you to solve more expensive problems than the competition can.

Indeed, paid employment is the playing field in which we take our clients' or employers' problems and provide our solutions in exchange, with financial rewards in the middle.

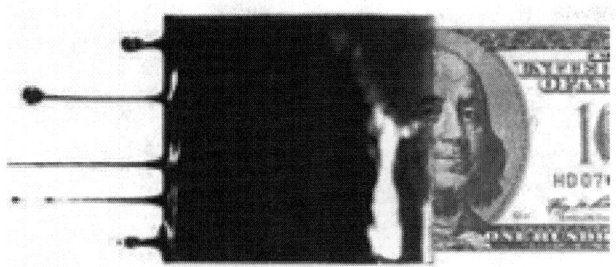

When we got to New York, we were amazed at how crazy people were acting all over the city. I'm not just talking about the taxi drivers; it happened at the airport, the hotel, the cafes and the shops everything felt like a marathon. Those of us who were there to run all had the same look; without saying anything we knew that we would be meeting at the starting line on Sunday. We were part of a conspiracy against adversity. We were a special club, and stood out from everything else. There were lots of fools walking the streets of the Big Apple in stylish coats, but wearing a pair of tennis shoes that they were breaking in. On the street, we walked past all the temptations imaginable: greasy fritangas, junk food, tobacco products, all qualities and vintages of wine, and billboards announcing midnight shows. Yet the runners of the world resisted: our big celebration would be Sunday at noon.

A worker or laborer solves problems that don't require a specialist; a technician has more skills and abilities because he or she knows how to solve more difficult and more expensive issues, and therefore also charges more than an unskilled worker, just as an engineer charges more than a technician because of their ability to solve bigger problems. When you prepare professionally for a future career, your bet is that you are preparing yourself with the knowledge and theory to be able to solve problems that not just anyone can solve.

Thus, in emerging and struggling economies such as those of many Latin American countries, a person with a university degree can earn around a 35% higher salary than a person who doesn't hold a degree. In that sense, your degree would offer you 35% more value and a 35% raise as compared to others in the workforce, just by having it. Yet the salaries available in emerging economies are so bad and so low that even adding an additional 35% to the full salary, isn't enough to represent a real advantage as far as being a "Young Talent," because what you can hope to earn is still not enough to get there.

A recent graduate accepts such salary conditions for 2 reasons:

a. There is an enormous amount of competition. There are so many candidates who want the same position under the self-imposed expectation that, once they get a foot in the door with that company, they will look for a way to climb in the job and salary ladder.

b. They know or have a sense that the theoretical knowledge they absorbed in school gives them the ability to solve problems, but they understand that they don't have the practical experience yet, which is what the employer or client really rewards, so they decide to start from the bottom with starvation wages so they can build the real skills and abilities they'll need to solve problems.

When running a marathon, you must change your attitude and outlook throughout the journey because the further you advance, the bigger the obstacles you will face. You must adapt to survive in other climates and run at different altitudes than you're used to, your nerves can get the best of you, and the risks that you must face logically and with intelligence can determine whether you finish the course with dignity or if you might even face death. The paradox is that you must train 1 hour every day for the hardest part of the marathon: the last hour of the race.

If you want to earn more money . . . find and solve more difficult problems.

No employer or client will pay you just for having a college degree. The market already pays 35% more to college grads than to non-grads. But what the market pays instead is for the solution to its problems.

Unfortunately, the current economic situation in most countries with emerging economies means that thousands— perhaps millions—of young people stay at entry levels, barely surviving in their sad and dismal routine, hoping that they will someday be promoted to a better position with a bigger salary, but not really understanding that the chances of them getting a professional promotion depends on them and them alone, and will happen only by focusing more proactively on the solutions they're offering their employer or client rather than merely on how long they've worked there.

This notion and its uncompromising reality catches millions of young people off guard—the market absorbs talent, sometimes it even pays for it, but there are so many young people trying to get up the ladder that the law of nature ends up putting everyone in their place. Employers simply wait, sometimes with a lot of anxiety, for new talents appear on the market because they need them to solve their problems.

That's why it's not uncommon to find talent scouts around who are willing to recruit the most advanced students from the most serious universities in the world; Those who demonstrate these problem-solving abilities, are able to land well-paying jobs that pay far above the average and receive offers even months before finishing their degrees, and if they don't, they still aren't too worried; they are clearly aware that entrepreneurship will always be an option for them—they will either find an employer or clients to purchase their practical solutions.

The reality for you is that, without question, one way or another the competition will be fierce. You'll be competing against thousands of other young people, as well as thousands of not so young employees, who want the same opportunity that you do to demonstrate they can find solutions to their employer's or client's problems; with thousands of young people who hope to shine if offered such an opportunity and thousands who, due to the saturation of the market, will not even receive an interview for the position.

A Colombian friend told me that he was shocked at the level of study required for jobs in Mexico because, each time he visited the country, a new taxi driver would take him from the airport to his hotel and all of them, according to him, had a bachelor's degree.

What my friend thought was that, to be a taxi driver in Mexico, at least in the tourism sector, the application required a university degree.

He told me this story with the upmost objectivity, and thought it was a positive reflection on the country that its Ministry of Tourism was aware that tourism brings millions of dollars in income to Mexico.

What my friend couldn't have imagined was that his taxi drivers' university educations were not Ministry of Tourism requirements, but a sad consequence of the rampant underemployment in my beloved Mexico. Young and not so young university students who don't find jobs where they can productively practice their professions end up as taxi drivers—with no disrespect to this respectable profession. But the basic idea here is that problem-solving is what creates wealth.

Oh! The sad truth is . . .

Anyone with a driver's license can solve his or her passengers' problem in this line of work. At least in theory, the drivers my friend mentioned should have the skills to solve other types of problems as well, and definitely be able to take on more "expensive" issues than those of running a taxi service.

And here, of course, we have two alternatives: the first is to rant against the government and its inability to generate an inclusive, productive, fast-paced economy—a whole long laundry list of complaints that goes on and on and which a leftist candidate could include in their campaign speech. You will excuse me for not taking that route, but I promised you at the beginning of the book to be objective and realistic.

The other alternative is to understand these taxi drivers' inability to find solutions to more expensive problems despite their university educations.

And it is that, if we acknowledge that the country's capacity to generate "abundance" is not enough to solve the economic reality of those taxi drivers, we must also conclude that if they didn't find other opportunities, it's surely because they aren't able to find them as hundreds of others do manage to find work in their fields. Perhaps they have struggled to find problems to solve; or worse yet, they don't know how to solve them.

The fact that this happens in some cases doesn't necessarily mean that it will happen to you; whether or not the country generates opportunities and wealth, you would not have to end up working in a trade when you've already prepared to practice a profession, but be careful—accumulating knowledge doesn't necessarily prepare you to work in the career you studied for, but rather to apply that knowledge to practical situations you may encounter once on the job.

In the end, the difference between the young person who has just finished their career and already has a desk in the Talent Development Program of some multinational corporation, and the many others who end up as taxi drivers after 27 months of not finding a job, began to take shape right there in the classrooms and not in the socioeconomic environment of the country.

I'll share the data I have about Mexico

as an example, but I assure you that in terms of percentages, these statistics won't be too different from those of other Latin American countries.

Mexico is widely criticized for its individualistic attitude in sports. They say that we are a powerhouse—but in any discipline that doesn't involve playing as a team. A few examples, we excel at: diving, weightlifting, middle-distance racing, running marathons, golf, sprinting, cycling, Tae Kwon Do, skating, and boxing.

I believe that the problem doesn't lie in our determination or in our willingness to take individual risks, but in the all too common "crab phenomenon," in which we always try to stop the others from crawling out of the bucket because we blame them for our fears and lack of competence.

You can't afford to wait until after you graduate to start focusing. You should take advantage of your university training, but also keep one eye focused on the type of problems that you would like to solve for an employer or client in the future; and just knowing that you are well prepared, you'll have better luck going out into the job market and competing for your space in it.

Chapter NINE

Your career: Against whom
and against how many are you
competing in this race? And there
go your numbers . . .

Hold on. There you go . . . Just another number . . .

As I finish the first edition of this book, we're now in the fourth quarter of 2010. Mexico just conducted its latest Population and Housing Census, which will be our source of statistics and data for the next 4 years; therefore, the information I'm providing is based on the 2009 census, in which 103 million people reported that they lived in the country. Shall we round it to **100 million** so we can talk in terms of round numbers?

About **40%** of Mexicans live in extreme poverty—which rules them out as your competitors; you've already left them behind, or rather, your parents did by positioning you in the reality that is your situation today.

Then around **47 million** people make up the economically active working population; that is, with everything happening in the country and the levels of poverty, only 4 out of 10 Mexicans work, and 4 out of 10 also support others on their paychecks, including older family members, children, sick relatives, or ones who are lazy.

So then Mexico has a **deficit** of about **2.8 million** jobs, in addition to the gap that grows each year between the number of young people who actively seek to enter the workforce and the number of jobs that the economy manages to create.

Therefore if, to give you another example, in **2010** we had close to **2.5** million jobs plus about **300 thousand young people** about to graduate—2.8 million jobs to fill by the end of the year—less the jobs the country has managed to create. We might optimistically hope to close out a record year with **500 thousand new jobs**, which means that the formal employment deficit will be 2.3 millions.

2.3 million young people, with a university degree or not, who will not be able to land a formal job.

I'm being generous in suggesting these numbers, and not going to tell you that you'll be competing against those 2.3 million people. Let's assume that, in an ideal and almost fantasy world, the very fact that you are studying, receiving a university education, and about to graduate means you have already put yourself ahead of millions of Mexicans on the competitors' list. Let's suppose that your university degree alone exonerates you from the conditions of inequity, injustice, or inability of the government's economy to generate sources of employment.

However, of those 500,000 jobs available, fewer than 200,000 actually require a college degree, which in any case shows a deficit of 100,000 jobs per year with a professional career track. Wow. If we were to play musical chairs, 100,000 young people this year will be left without a job-chair in the formal economy.

You may be thinking that you'll always have

the chance to play musical job-chairs again next year with the new positions that are generated, but let me remind you that colleges and universities will also be graduating another 300 or 310 thousand new graduates, so the reality is that there will be 100,000 university graduates underemployed this year and as many more the next year, and that many other graduates who will be facing unemployment are on their way— who knows how many others will inevitably join those waiting to start their career? You know what happens to the value of a tomato when there are a lot of tomatoes on the market? It decreases.

So many graduates are looking for jobs and waiting to be employed that the market value of their solutions to problems diminishes. If apart from all this we've already established that having a degree does not necessarily enable them to offer tangible solutions to their employers' or clients' problems, let's add the competition variable. Even if you believe that you are very efficient, the value that the market will pay for your solutions goes down due to the mere presence of the thousands of competitors.

But, in addition, there is also the variable of quality of your competitors. You are not competing against just any dimwit. Here are some other numbers for you . . . .

For one «Young Talent» to emerge from the pack, approximately 3,000 young people need to enroll.

And here's another fact: out of every 100 students who start university in Mexico, only 22 finish, of which 18 will graduate. Of every 100 who finish and graduate, only 20 successfully complete a postgraduate degree, and out of every 100 who finish their professional training with a master's, only 2, on average, immediately land a career track position that admits them into the «Young Talent» club.

Many others will continue growing and developing to meet the definition of someone who has improved their standard of living in a comprehensive way by applying what they've learned in college to their life, but only 2 are already at that level just after they've graduated.

If my math doesn't fail me . . .

Started College	Completed College with a:	
100	18	Bachelor's degree
550	20	Postgraduate degree
2750	2	Young Talent

These may seem like cold, hard numbers and at first be shocking, but if we deviate a little further—if we take the sample from those who start high school and consider that out of every 100, only 25 start university, we would then need to start with 5,500 students to find a single «Young Talent».

So now, and only for those who like to feel important, let's say you've been to college and already graduated; in that alone, you've left millions of people in the dust who simply didn't even start; tens of thousands who stopped after junior high, thousands who stopped at high school, and you are now competing against hundreds at your same level.

But there's one thing that complicates the equation: globalization. It turns out that today, out of every 10 top executives in Mexico . . .

Three are foreign nationals—and this trend is increasing.

Globalization instantly added difficulty to competition in the labor market, raised the level of demand, and changed the market standard. While young Mexicans are thinking of voting for contestants at La Academia or Latin American

Idol (and I say "vote" with sadness here, they aren't even dreaming of participating because they know their talent level isn't high enough or are too lazy to audition), young Japanese, Indians, Chinese, and many Central Americans are not worrying about themselves and their egos, but instead focusing on refining the skills they intend to offer the job market when they graduate.

The conditions in Mexico City, and of this entire nation in general, are inhospitable for the average runner. The altitude, the pollution, and the lack of support from other people make the street a real training ground. Curiously, the most outstanding runners in the world come from Africa to train in Mexico, as they find the terrain so challenging. Anyone who makes it in Mexico can make it anywhere.

We have let our efforts be diffused because of a crisis—first an economic one, and then a crisis of leadership and values. The feelings of apathy and discouragement are so acute that it's left many of your colleagues in a state of paralysis, unable to advance not only in their careers, but also in their own lives. The thing is that in a few years, they'll have no choice but to go out—whether or not they're depressed—get to work and provide what their families need, and they will come face to face with all the competitors that I've just described.

> *Why should I hire a Mexican worker who is late, badly dressed, makes spelling errors, and complains that the office is too far away, when I could instead hire a Chinese employee who is more highly qualified, has an excellent attitude, doesn't mind coming from the other side of the world to work for me, and will cost me the same or a little less to hire?*

Mexico 1

For every "Young Talent" Mexico produces:

China	India	United States	European Union
1,300	1,100	700	400

Up until this point, we've only been considering what it will take for you to compete against 3,500 other Mexicans for a job! Can you imagine the competition you'll face at the international level when you leave college? Do you realize the level of competition you'll face in the world market when you finish your academic training and start the real race?

It means that to be on equal footing internationally and come up with 3,500 talents, Mexico will have to produce something like nine million six hundred thousand young people. And it's not only because these other countries are more efficient at producing talent, but also because they have so many young people to train. What if I ask you to count a billion Chinese students? Even if the Chinese are just as efficient or inefficient at producing talents as we are, their sheer numerical advantage is overwhelming. Considering another aspect of the "quality" of our competitors; they perhaps have more awareness of when they're being stupid, and that young people in other countries understand very early on that if they don't focus and take advantage of their university education 100% from day one, they'll be out of the running as far as any possibility of aspiring to and having a minimum quality of life.

Due to overpopulation, Chinese children prepare and develop their abilities to the maximum, since they know that they'll one day have to support their aging parents; so from an early age, they're required to create mental structures based on proactivity, productivity, problem-solving, logic, and critical thinking, arithmetic, art, and music. What do you think of it?

About 10 or 15 years ago, my generation didn't even talk about any of these things. What did it matter to my colleagues and to me whether or not a lot of Chinese people lived half way around the world? There was no way it would affect us! Today, globalization and global technologies have promoted everyone so they can compete on the same playing field; and with this they've raised competition's level of quality tremendously.

Employers or clients will not have ethnic

preferences or be biased toward foreign candidates. What they're looking for are practical and efficient solutions to their problems and needs, and they'll pay whoever can give it to them. I'll say this as directly as possible: they will hire the best talent that they can afford, and since there are so many candidates to choose from, they surely won't have to pay too much.

Back in my time, the Chinese "threat" to the market was mainly due to imported products sold on the street; many businesses began to disappear because cheaper goods arrived from the Asian continent. Though it's true that the quality of these products was sometimes dubious, the fact is that the market began to consume them more than ones produced nationally. As the quality of these Chinese products continued getting better, thousands of Mexican companies went bankrupt and closed. Today you still find finished Chinese products that are higher quality, and being sold at a lower price than the raw materials would cost to produce them in Mexico. Hundreds of manufacturers who used to produce items have now become importers, but still earn more money than they did making products.

Of course, production and manufacturing operations and the jobs they produce continue to grow—but on the other side of the world—at least that was the case when I was young . . . but now, your generation faces an even harder situation. Asia and the developed countries are not only exporting very high-quality products abroad, they are also exporting their "Young Talent," a perfectly well-qualified and highly trained workforce that is also used to charging very little for their services and are extremely efficient. You can, of course, rest on your laurels and think that what I'm describing here won't affect you, but you may also choose to see this as an issue and start worrying about or dealing with the problem before you have to face it.

Of course—and to make matters worse—I must remind you that all those people who came onto the job market before you and now have a job or business of their own, also want to pay the rent and feed their families, so they will do whatever it takes to keep their positions or clients.

And not only that, of course they also want to grow in their careers and to live better! So as soon as you finish celebrating because you've landed a job or started getting clients, you'll find competitors who are already far ahead of you as far as practical experience and their positioning in the market who want to keep their lead. By already having more time on the market, they are more valuable than you; their solutions to employers' or clients' problems are more efficient and optimal because their services are more fine-tuned.

If you were an employer or client and had to decide between hiring someone else or you, and both you and the other candidate have exactly the same credentials . . . who would you logically choose? Using the same criteria, who would you pay more?

My grandmother told me 20 years ago: "Find something that you like to do and that you are better at doing than 10,000 other people, and it will always go well for you." What she didn't know was that the world would become what it is today, and that the employment outlook would change so much. By 2025, you will have to find something that you like to do and are better at than two hundred thousand people to make sure that you will really do well in life.

Well, by now I would only need some depressing music to slit your wrists to. I know that the last 4 pages must have seemed like they were taken out of the *Divine Comedy*, right from the fourth ring of hell. I wanted to make things look grim . . . nearly impossible.

Why? Because in the first place, you can bet that the situation is even more serious than I'm making it sound. Secondly, with my objective being to make your tooth hurt before it's necessary to remove it, I want to propose, without lecturing you, that you should reconsider some things about your daily habits and behavior while you're still in college, and think a little more deeply about preparing to face and confront the inevitable reality that awaits you.

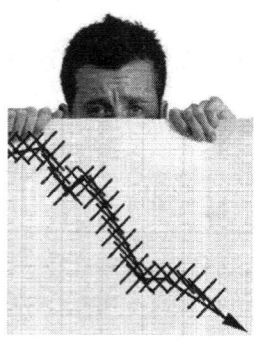

Both the winner of the marathon and the runner who finishes last have to travel the same path, the same distance, and will see the same landscape. The only thing that's different about these two runners is their objectives. And although Mexican runners have long been a major force in long distance racing, more and more African colleagues are receiving sponsorships for their enviable athletic performances, as well as placing in the top positions as far as the world ranking.

Chapter TEN

Another dose of reality . . . putting them through college

Our Latinx culture, and more specifically our Mexican culture, places economic and patrimonial value on two things that are considered life's priorities: owning a home and giving our children the opportunity to earn a college degree.

It makes no difference that in some instances, buying a home means dealing with bandits who sell mortgages with interest rates in excess of 40% per year for 40 years, and that at the end of the term your house is not worth half of what you owe only in interest. Still, people feel that making the effort to buy their own home is worth it.

It does not matter if for 10 years they have paid twice as much in interest as they would have paid in rent, or that the first 25 years of the loan they aren't paying anything toward capital; their idiosyncratic logic tells them that it's better to own a home.

I don't want to dismiss the excellent real estate agencies and the conditions they offer so that thousands of people can purchase assets, I'm only referring to the fact that there are extreme cases in the market and reputable people who operate and offer coverage or over-valued assets relying on the guise of popular belief and culture.

At the same time, you can find cases like that of Doña Margarita, who being a single mother, has literally dedicated her life to raising her three children and has promised to give them all the opportunity to study for a career, despite her inhumane work days and all the deprivation and sacrifice it will take. "Seeing them through college, parents, means leaving them with something."

Nor should the scene be overly dramatic; any middle and even upper-class father or mother goes to sleep happily knowing that "I'm not going to leave them a large fortune, but my inheritance will be to leave them with an education."

Well I'm sorry to tell you that, economically speaking, a college degree doesn't guarantee you any kind of practical claim on wealth.

Again the phrase: "People won't pay you for

what you know, but for what you do with what you know" comes to mind. As we've previously established, thousands of young people leave college and sell their time and knowledge for less than what their parents paid for their monthly tuition, and the problem is exactly that: they sell their time and knowledge, not a solution for problems that their employers or clients have.

In the end, your parents may have made every sacrifice so you could succeed, but what will end up actually impacting your life will be the accumulation of decisions and actions that you take, and nothing else.

A backhanded slap

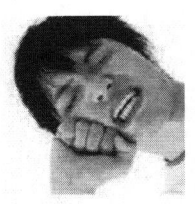

The United Nations (UN), proposed the idea that in 2025, being "illiterate" will include those who do not speak English and haven't mastered use of a computer.

By 2035 the average executive, that is, even a mediocre one, will speak his native language, English, and Chinese, and a brilliant executive will know at least two more languages.

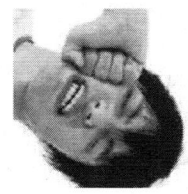

As Bill Gates says, "If you finished your college education two years ago, you've prepared yourself for a world that no longer exists."

The fact is that 80% of tomorrow's careers don't even exist yet, the world's problems at that point in the future are still largely unknown; that is, you'll have to be prepared to solve problems that don't yet exist.

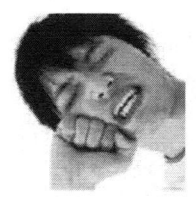

Our world updates the technology it requires every two years so that 50% of what you've learned will already be a part of mainstream technology just three years later.

Chapter ELEVEN

What should you do about it and what should you stop doing about it?

know I've given you a harsh scenario that is fairly discouraging. Anyone hearing this might give up from the get-go, before even trying. I've described the brutal competition you'll face, and a playing field so rough, that you might well feel like going off on a tangent and asking yourself: What's the point in even studying? Why put the effort into finishing my degree if, even upon graduating, I won't be even close to the strongest candidates? I'm just going to leave school right now and go into the business informally."

But this type of thinking could occur only if you have a mindset that allows for mediocrity. Anyone who turns back when they're already halfway to their goal only "half believes" in themselves.

If that's your way of thinking, if you really believe that it makes no difference whether or not you continue because the description of the reality that awaits you is so painful, it wouldn't even be worth my time to waste this paper painting that picture for you; it would be the same thing as giving importance to a weak brain rooted in mediocrity. If that's the case, feel free to treat me the same way—toss me, and everything I've said, into the trash can, including my book. May your life go as well as possible— all the best and God bless you.

You see, I know a lot of people 20 years older than me, and many of them have told me that, through the years, they remember one or two books that they read in their youth that gave them a different perspective on their existence, served as a counterbalance in their decision-making, and thus changed their lives.

I can remember at least three monumental books from when I was younger that played a part in my life. But none of these books, and none of these people ever said: "I quit studying and allowed my life to fall into mediocrity because I read a book." To the contrary, of the books that make a difference in your life, you will remember the ones that showed you something completely different from your perspective or showed you the same reality, but in a different way. My goal, as I stated in the introduction, is to make the effort to tell you the things that I would like a stranger to tell my children when they're your age. And, of course, not to leave them feeling defeated before they've even started off, but to inspire them and warn them about the pigs on the road ahead.

While it's true that the reality I've described is harsh, it's also true that we still haven't actually talked about you yet. The extent of your abilities will be what is measured against that future reality, and the magnitude of your skills that will determine whether the competition looks threatening, friendly, or even encouraging. For some, life will even be easy and full of opportunities; it all depends on what you are made of; and more than that: your awareness of your own abilities and talents.

Meanwhile, let me give you an idea of what you can't do about the employment situation and what—from my point of view—you in fact can do.

Always avoid:

1. Giving up and giving in mid-race—or in the middle of your studies—simply because it seems too difficult.

2. Wasting time being immature and wasting the extraordinary opportunity you have today to receive a university education. I don't care

if your parents, the state, or you yourself pay for it.

3. Being happy when the university "goes on strike," when a mediocre teacher misses or cancels a class and gives you "time-out," or when a classmate, who is ignorant and unaware offers to exchange grades for drinks.

4. Allowing your college experience to be wasted—either because of you, your teachers, or the institution where you're studying.

5. Thinking that this stage of your life ends when you receive your degree and to focus on such an elementary objective assures that you will achieve equally "basic" results in life. Don't just study to pass an exam, absorb the knowledge you receive and integrate it into your life so that you can learn to retain it, appropriate it, make it yours, and have it on hand when you need to use it to sell solutions to your employer or client. If you aim at a hanging fruit with a stone, you may hit the ground, but if you want to hit that treetop, you must aim for the moon.

6. Taking your college education lightly;

take advantage of it, leave the dumb stuff behind you.

7. Becoming a nerd with the idea that the only important thing at this point in your life is theoretical knowledge, because this is not true. Your professional studies as you prepare for a future career is important, but your youth is too. Have fun while you go through this training; you can find a balance between enjoying life at your age, being young, and adding professionalism and seriousness to your career.

8. Not having fun on your career run. Think of a football player who is going to play the Super Bowl; preparing for this game is serious business, but if you don't have fun on the road, you may lose the game.

9. Going light on yourself—if you know you can give yourself more, do it. In your training, in your life, in your relationships, in your daily existence, constantly challenge yourself—only by giving your very best can you find and receive the best in life.

10. Losing your focus: If the captain of a ship changes the angle of the rudder only two degrees and then takes a nap, when they wake up they will realize that they've

veered thousands of miles off course from their destination. A small innocent deviation multiplied over a significant period of time leads to a life completely different from what we dreamed of when we were 17 years old.

What you can do is:

1. Anticipate the future.

2. Develop a specialty.

3. Stay focused.

4. Practice a systematic method of study that leads to results in your daily life.

5. Develop your problem-solving abilities.

6. Develop both social and interpersonal skills.

7. Market your skills, not your knowledge.

8. Aim for the stars.

9. Explore entrepreneurship.

10. Go for it . . . you're well prepared to run this race and give it your best!

11. Never stop training for the race.

1. Anticipate the future

Remember the analogy we made earlier using the New York City Marathon? You can't start preparing for the race on the day of it; the type of training practice you decide to establish months earlier must be in keeping with your goal. Imagine for a moment if you only had the opportunity to start running two hours before the race? Would your odds of winning it improve?

NYC Marathon 2008. Greenbox

It's counterproductive when young people, recent graduates naively keep saying that they can't understand how potential employers could be looking for "recent graduates" who also have "two-years of experience in a similar position." Of course if your peers haven't done their homework, such a job description would seem like a joke.

The worst thing about it is that this is the attitude that thousands of young people project when faced with their inability to find employment, not a job that pays well, just a job.

The keyword here is **anticipating**.

The answer is obvious; my 8-year-old son knows it (and I know he does because I've asked him): How can you be a recent graduate and have two years of experience working in a similar position? By starting the process of accumulating work experience two years before graduation.

In college, you acquire knowledge; on the street you gain experiences. And I've chosen *experiences* in the plural, instead of *experience*, on purpose. Some people can work at a job for 20 years and have only one year of experience, that is, they learned things for one year and have been repeating what they discovered in that first year 20 more times. Your employer or client will pay for your problem-solving skills; therefore, the training you receive in the classroom must be adjusted to fit everyday life, since that's where the problems that will need to be solved arise. The speed with which problems and their solutions change is several times faster than the speed with which universities update their curriculum, so the only possible way to graduate and at the same time stay up to date is to anticipate what is coming and start preparing for a "similar position" (which will ask for experience in the job description) a few years before graduating.

You'll find good reasons—and many opportunities—to do this: you're in the classroom, your perspective will change dramatically, you'll become more demanding of yourself as a student and more selective about the amount and type of information that you take in and appropriate. Since you won't necessarily be working for the money, but rather, as a practical complement to your professional training, you can afford to seek out positions you want and openings in companies that you want to work for—as long as you do a good job of "selling" your proposal, it will be much easier to place yourself as a volunteer than as an employee.

After working there a few months, if you really contribution to the company in question, they will make you a job offer; if not, it does not matter, they will certainly reward you with a letter of recommendation and you can use this to demonstrate experiences.

Perhaps working there will delay your graduation a year, perhaps even up to 18 months, since it will surely be very difficult for you to fulfill both your work and academic commitments well—but believe me, it is worth it. Consider these jobs like practice labs; the most important thing here is that you'll have a chance to calibrate your knowledge in an everyday setting. Let me also mention that some college students must work while in school to support themselves—they've already learned to balance this kind of schedule and it hasn't been impossible for them. My respect and admiration go out to all of you who are already doing this.

2. Develop a specialty

Specialization enables the professionalization of the knowledge you've obtained. To specialize is basically to make yourself "special," and therefore, to stand out.

With all the information you've read so far in this book, I'm sure I don't need to stress the point too much that your university education isn't really the thing that will make you stand out; what will really get you ahead and to the starting line, and assure you a better place in the real competition, doesn't end with a bachelor's degree. It comes down to a question of basic math.

How can you stand out and be "special" among 300 thousand other young people who've graduated the same year as you in the same country? Having a specialization makes you stand out, elevates you above your entire generation, and also gives you a stronger candidate profile.

On average, anyone with a master's degree can expect to earn between 25% and 40% more working in the same position, but better still, they are promoted 18 months sooner, on average, and to higher-level positions.

On the other hand, specialization is not only obtained by pursuing a postgraduate degree; the basic concept is to make yourself special so that you stand out among thousands of other people. Of course, continuing with a higher-level academic degree is also a pathtoward developing a specialty, but not the only one.

The combination of knowledge and experiences that you will accumulate by anticipating the future will help you develop your abilities, to explore your talents in more depth, and to discover not only what you're good at, but also what you would be very mediocre at doing on the job and what you most like to do. You must choose your vocation, and not the other way around. When you find that you enjoy one activity over another. Once you discover the types of problems that you're passionate about solving, you'll have an extraordinary advantage over your entire generation, since you'll not only be working with the necessary theory and knowledge, but also, with all the passion you have. And this may mean that you will be able to focus on your daily tasks.

3. Stay focused. Focus the best of yourself on a single point

The sun is the maximum source of energy in our system of life. In fact, our planet is part of the solar system, whose name comes from recognizing the sun as its source of energy, without which life on our planet would be nonexistent.

In Desenfocus. Greenbox.

If we hold a fragile and thin sheet of paper to the sky under the constant glare of the sun, what happens to it? Our first thought might be that it would start to burn! But think again, would it really burn? The answer is no. If we keep exposing the sheet of paper to the sun, perhaps in 6 or 7 months it would turn yellow and dry out; but even after a couple of years it would not generate a combustion and catch fire on its own, despite having fuel, oxygen, and heat.

For the sheet of paper to catch fire, one more element is needed . . . focus. If we place a magnifying glass between the sun and the sheet of paper, this leads to a concentration of a tiny, miniscule, amount of energy on a specific point, and therefore causes combustion and starts a fire. The sun, the maximum source of energy in our life system, is incapable of generating the minimum response if we don't focus its energy.

Once you know what you want to specialize in, you have discovered the best part of you and can focus your own energies on that single point. There's no doubt that, like the sun, you are a constant and fantastic source of light and energy. With your abilities, your professionalism, your knowledge, your creativity, and your enthusiasm, you can surely achieve anything you want, but like a sunbeam . . . you need a focus.

I'm not saying that it's impossible for you to accomplish four things at the same time, but it is much, much more difficult to achieve all them together than one by one.

As the old adage goes: "He who tries to grab too much can't hold onto anything;" therefore, you must focus.

On the other hand, being focused doesn't mean becoming an antisocial, isolated, and completely celibate zombie. I know people who don't even allow themselves a break to have coffee with friends because, according to them, they don't want to get distracted from their studies.

Focusing means finding the best part of you and focusing all your energies around it in the same place, not isolating yourself or feeling blue throughout your youth because you've taken this exercise in concentration too far.

You can perfectly well participate in a variety of different activities as long as they allow you to explore different facets of your life and you are clear about your goals. So if you also want to join a sports team on your campus, earn a scholarship for 10 hours a week, and have the best GPA in your class, you may find it difficult to excel at all three things. I'm not telling you to stop doing one activity or another, but rather suggesting you should clarify your goals and expectations for each of the three. Of course you can do all three, but with a clear idea of what you should focus on . . . if your life goal isn't to receive a university scholarship and travel abroad as a college athlete, then simply enjoy sports activities 100% while lowering your expectations as you play. Be clear about your priorities at this moment in your life and arrange your activities according to the order of the priorities you've established whenever you're able. If you become aware that you need to cancel any of your activities right off the bat, do so and stay focused.

4. Practice a systematic study method that leads to results in your daily life

Because of a distortion of the educational model used in developing countries and because of a cultural attachment to the path of least resistance, most young people have learned to apply their efforts based on short-term vision.

Let me give you a realistic example: of course your grandparents and your grandparents' parents were thrifty. You don't really know how much they had or where they kept it, but they always had a safety net in case of emergencies; they were just brought up that way.

On the other hand, you're likely to have observed that your parents are always struggling to systematically save a portion of their income. There is always a good reason not to put money aside, even though we know that by setting aside a tiny daily savings, we will ensure a peaceful retirement in our old age.

My friends would make fun of me because I ran in tights to protect myself from the cold, I smeared myself with Vaseline, and put Band-Aids on my nipples to avoid them rubbing on my clothes. The girls were freaked out when I would do an hour of aerobics or Zumba with them; they didn't even flirt with me. Swimming on Sunday afternoons instead of napping or watching football wasn't so bad, but having my chest and armpits shaved was. That was simply the way a determined runner looked.

What I want to say is that in the days when your parents were children, they learned that money lost all its value if they kept it, literally a television could cost 20% or 30% more the following weekend if the economic crises and devaluations and other economic phenomena so determined. Your parents learned (and we learned) to have short-term financial visions; whereas your grandparents learned that they could literally bury their money in the backyard of the house and it would still have the same value, or even be worth a little more in the future.

No wonder our grandparents had long-term value beliefs, long-term life plans, long-term marriages and friendships, long lives and health that lasted.

Meanwhile, the dominant social norms

when you were a child trained you to think in the short term; your brain learned to study in order to pass the next exam and nothing else; so the information you come in contact with accumulates in your short-term memory and is not related to any practical function—and then it's forgotten.

Think of your brain as a computer: if you try to store everything on your hard drive you will eventually slow down the system. I know that devices with almost unlimited storage have now been invented, and in fact your brain works like that; however, can you actually read each and every file that is saved on your hard drive? How long would it take you? Would it make any sense to do that? Of course, knowing where the information is when you need it is enough, right?

Well, with your college preparation and experience, something similar begins to happen; the information that you don't relate in any meaningful way to your daily life or use as the possible solution to your employer's or client's problems of your employer or client will simply be added to your short-term memory and then forgotten; it will be very useful on the day of the exam, but will eventually become buried in a deeper part of your brain and discarded not long afterwards.

Just as you sometimes defrag your laptop's hard drive, lose information due to a virus, update and perhaps even accidentally delete your folders, your brain also manages the information it receives every day.

So if I challenged you right now to remember how you solved those third-grade math problems you enjoyed so much in grade school, you might not have any idea at all how you did that (at least this has happened to me); therefore, don't bet on your hard drive, but on your processor.

Here is a reminder of the importance of having work experiences while you are studying to complete the last semesters of your college degree, you will have the opportunity to turn the information you receive into something meaningful in the classroom and in everyday life, reinforcing your understanding in the process, but beyond that, be able to collect all your professional resources into one dynamic toolbox, having those tools on hand later to solve your employer's or client's real problems.

Look far into the distance.

Even if you have run thousands of times, have "taken care" of your body, are highly motivated, have the best tennis shoes and the best lucky charm, you will not know how well prepared you were to run the marathon until you've crossed the finish line.

5. Develop your problem-solving abilities

Like it or not, the life that awaits you will be governed by fierce competition. The competitors who know how to solve problems will stand out. You will never be sufficiently prepared for life until you start living it.

If couples waited until they were truly ready to start families, there would be no population explosion. The truth is that you aren't ready for 70% of the things in life until you start doing them. The good thing about this is that you can proactively anticipate the future, then specialize and focus on those 30% of things that you can be prepared for.

When you have a baby and she needs milk at three in the morning, you won't be able to give her "a copy of your classmate's test," you won't be able to ask your mom to "take the notes for you," and of course, you won't be able to ask God to call an "infant strike" at that moment so that you can postpone finding a solution to your problems for a few weeks. You will have to get milk and to figure out a solution, plain and simple.

Remember that we have already established that: "People aren't paid for what they know, but for what they do with what they know." Surely you've known people who weren't that bright or at least didn't seem to be because they were such deadbeats and wouldn't even stay up all night before exams . . . and yet they have advanced further in their lives and in their careers in a couple of years, than most advance in decades.

Look at them, try to find success factors and you will realize that what really makes the difference is that they solve problems for others, preferably expensive problems or many different problems, but problems.

Of course they don't use all the knowledge they acquired through their university degrees, but when they need it, they "know where they left it." They become indispensable to their employers or clients, therefore, they receive larger paychecks from them.

> *We were crossing the Queensboro Bridge to Manhattan, after having run around 14 miles, when someone yelled at us: "Hey, Mexicans, move, move!" (Get out of our way, Mexicans; we're going first!) Obediently we stepped aside, but a bit confused and also feeling offended. We were being overtaken by 2 runners who were moving faster than us. They seemed to pass us hand in hand, although in reality it was a band that kept them connected. One was blind; the other was helping him achieve his goal. At that moment, Felipe Senior and I said to each other: "We have no reason to block their way."*

6. Develop both social and interpersonal skills

"Those who went to college five years ago were preparing for a world that no longer exists," said Bill Gates when explaining the overwhelming speed with which technology is updated and inevitably changes our daily lives.

And in fact, the world we were preparing for only a few years ago no longer exists; therefore, we must prepare ourselves for a world that doesn't yet exist and, better still, for the ones that will continue to exist for many years. That's why betting on the development of your social skills and on training is a safe bet. In 5 years, people will continue to be people; in 10 years, our computers may be tiny, telephones could be inserted into everyone's teeth, and perhaps we will have GPS locators implanted in our navels, allowing us, just by approaching the refrigerator, to create a grocery list of all the items we need to purchase that week according to our needs and history as consumers of food products.

The march of technology cannot be stopped, but people like you and me will continue to live with the effects of what we lacked in childhood, our personal traumas, our satisfied or unsatisfied desires, yearnings, dreams, frustrations, successes, joys, our sadness or depression, self-esteem, attitudes, passions or lack of love.

Your employer, your boss, your boss's boss's boss, as well as your internal or external clients, will continue being human—with human emotions and all too human needs. Any time and effort you invest in learning about those needs, understanding them and integrating them into your value proposition, will be very much in your favor. And the problems that you could end up solving for your employer or client may not be only technical or objective; problems always have an emotional element that lies in, and originates from, a human need.

Let me give you an example: if a lady in traffic blows a tire on her car at 11 a.m. in a safe and commercial part of the city, how much do you think she would be willing to pay someone to help her change it? How much of a hurry is she in? Well, how much more than the going rate would she pay to get the tire fixed in half the time? Now let's pretend that the same person has the same mishap, but at 8:30 at night in a highly dangerous area the city.

The problem is basically the same, don't you agree? In both cases the tire needs to be changed, and the woman (or client) either doesn't know how or doesn't want to or cannot change it alone; but what human and emotional needs are behind the tire in each example? Of course she would be willing to pay three, four, or five times more to have the tire changed in the second scenario because she is also terrified and trying to keep her fear under control, so if the service provider hurries, surely the customer will respond by giving them an additional tip.

Now if the worker who provides the service realizes the emotional state the woman is in, and lets her know that he is the gang leader of that neighborhood, and that everyone respects him, and that she's not in any danger as long as he is there with her, she will calm down knowing that she'll be on her way in a few minutes, safe and sound with a new tire ...

Surely you can see that the apparent problem has much more of a backstory to it than merely changing a tire. Likewise, the problems you specialize in solving will always have much more of an emotional background for your employers or clients than you merely finding the solutions.

So, if the cardiologist saves your life because he is an excellent doctor, you thank her, but if she also makes you feel calm, explains the process, treats you respectfully and empathizes with your situation, surely you will be more likely to recommend her even more highly.

If the person selling you children's shoes, in addition to providing you with excellent service, also gives you a little lollipop for your child, you are drawn in; if your waiter, in addition to bringing you the soup, also makes you feel important, you are more likely to go back to that restaurant.

I could give thousands and thousands of other small examples. Developing your social skills is essential.

In 2008, I saw for the first time the summary of a study carried out by world employment leader ManpowerGroup, one of the largest and most prominent staffing firms in the whole world. They had gone to employers, specifically those in Latin America, and asked them openly:

1. *What are the social skills that you consider essential for your jobs?*

2. *What do you look for in a candidate, besides knowing how to do what they are supposed to do?*

Here were the replies:

Teamwork	**38%**
Interpersonal Communication	**36%**
Personal relationships	**35%**
Decision-making skills	**33%**
Negotiation	**32%**
Leadership	**28%**
Creativity and innovation	**25%**
Management skills	**24%**
Implementation	**23%**
Written Communication	**21%**

This can give you an idea of where you should direct your attention, but the issue does not stop there, afterwards the same thousands of employers in Latin America were asked:

What abilities or social skills are hardest to find among the pool of candidates?

Guess what? The list is very similar:

Teamwork	**78%**
Interpersonal Communication	**73%**
Personal relationships	**69%**
Decision-making skills	**66%**
Negotiation	**57%**
Leadership	**55%**
Creativity and Innovation	**54%**
Management skills	**54%**
Implementation	**51%**
Written communication	**50%**

Can you see how tough this equation is? The social skills that employers or clients consider essential are precisely the ones that are most difficult to find. Knowing this can help us understand why we have people with deficiencies in their college education, even without a degree, leading high-performance teams in which most employees hold higher academic credentials than them.

Let me explain it this way: we've established that, year after year, universities graduate three hundred thousand young graduates with different vocations and specialties; that is, the fabric from which to cut select graduates. There are a lot to choose from, but how many of them know, for example, how to work on a team, communicate effectively with others, resolve conflicts, and create an energetic atmosphere with their colleagues? At the end of the day, if you take a graduate with high level social skills and another with high university credentials, it seems that the balance is tipped in favor of the former, because these are the candidates who are in short supply.

Let's understand that I'm not suggesting you throw away your education, stop studying, and take 16 courses in body language and motivation instead. No.

We have already established that all the trends indicate that university graduates earn between 25% and 40% more than non-grads;

what I'm suggesting you do is to turn yourself into a competitive candidate

If your employer or client sees that you are not only a qualified professional, but also a social professional with excellent people skills, then you can: not only charge for changing the tire, but also for solving the client's emotional problems. Both in the academic sense, as well as on a human and social level, you mustn't stop preparing and improving.

How can you tell a runner?

Their face looks strained when they are practicing their favorite sport, but they always greet other runners.

They have loose legs and prefer to walk rather than jumping in the car.

The first thing they do in the morning is empty their bowels. They are in tune with seconds, minutes, and

distance: they can run for an hour without a watch and also know how long a mile is.

7. Market your skills, not your knowledge

Returning to the concept of problem-solving, it is not enough for you to know how to fix the tire; even if you have developed the ability to strengthen the relationship with your client, it will be important that you know how to market this.

On the one hand, very few young people who start their career go out to sell what they can do based solely on what they know, they believe that they will be hired simply for knowing what they say they know; but the fact is that very few have any idea that they have to go out and market it. Our social stigma against salespersons is based on the stereotype of those who, having failed working at what they studied (if they actually ever studied), end up, much to their regret, selling something.

After a person has been on unemployment for 15 months, they begin to lower their expectations until they're finally willing to accept "even a job in sales." And if there is a choice between being a "salesperson or taxi driver," most would prefer to be a taxi driver; with all due respect to our drivers.

In our collective unconscious, we have in mind a profile of the seller as someone who must be an expert in manipulation in order to force the other person to part with their money in exchange for a product that they do not need. Nothing could be further from the truth.

The ability to sell is something like having a Doctorate of Skills and Social Skills. At the end of the day, we are all sellers; we all go about it according to how well or how badly we sell who we are and what we do.

A child sells his mother his; if she buys what he wants, then she has done so to satisfy him. A doctor sells her patients a treatment plan; it's not enough to sign the prescription, if the doctor doesn't sell her patients on the idea of being healed, then they will abandon the treatment without being cured, and will begin to speak badly of this doctor, who will then lose her patients and credibility.

The CEO of a company has to go out and "sell" the board of directors, for instance, the idea that it's going to take twenty-five million dollars to invest in the new project. Once the board has "bought" this idea, the CEO and her deputy directors then sell the idea about that new project to others who in turn will transfer the information down the line to the different levels within the company where the idea must be implemented. The tangible results delivered to the shareholders will depend on these necessary coworkers "buying" the idea with enthusiasm.

D.R. Bansky.

Yes, we are all salespeople: some for the better good, some for worse . . . some just managed to barely get something in exchange for something else; others selling what they have, not based on their university preparation or their social skills, but because of what they are able to sell their employer or client.

The president of any country in the world must first sell the idea of their leadership to the people so that they will vote for him or her; then they must sell all their initiatives to Congress or Parliament. The media or spin doctors eventually sell us the idea that this or that government is doing things right or messing things up, and we base our cultural heritage and social identity on the opinion that some public figure has been able to sell us.

I highly recommend investing time and money in developing your abilities and social skills. Be sure to keep reading as many books as you can, attend all the seminars and workshops that are available, or else accept temporary jobs while you're studying—including working in the field of sales, directly as a salesperson if you can.

> *If you are really interested in reading it, I would gladly give you my e-book. Don't sell me something . . . help me buy it; register on my social networks and request it by email, I'll send you a copy free of charge.*

> *Helios Herrera*

8. Aim for the stars

"If you're going to be thinking anyway, you might as well think big."

Rem Koolhaas.

"Think big and you will be big."

Donald Trump.

If you are preparing to finish the marathon, the best thing that can happen to you is for you to actually finish it; if you prepare to win it, the worst that can happen to you is to be among the finalists.

The cause of our mediocrity is precisely due to the fact that we prepare for so little; therefore, when we achieve very little, we are still "successful." But when we want a little more . . . we aren't prepared to achieve it or to make it a permanent part of our lives.

My focus for the past 22 years has been on linking human development tools to workplace productivity. I have given 1,500 seminars or conference lectures to a cumulative audience of two million people spanning several countries, and I have not met a single person who doesn't want more.

We all want and we all yearn for something more—more money, better living conditions, more health, excellent economy, more love; we all want more.

But in this physical world of equally physical realities "having desire to do something is not enough;" it only produces effects—only actions produce reactions.

The point is that if you don't start preparing from now on to achieve *more*; when you want it later on, you simply won't be able to have it, even if you really want it.

If most of our university education is spent studying only for short-term goals like passing the exam, when we face life five years later, we simply won't have the tools we need to find solutions to every problem. This is a simple and basic concept.

If your life goal, at least for now, is to be successful in your professional career, you have to prepare yourself to become the CEO of a transnational corporation. I'm not saying that upon graduation you will become one, but you must give yourself that much mental space to grow.

If we compare your professional career to a building and you expect to become a skyscraper or a modern "smart" building during your life, you must be prepared.

At this time in your life you are digging in the ground and building your foundation; it's a lot of work and more than 30% of the total cost of the building. Moreover, when the effort of laying the foundation is over, you return to level ground and ask yourself: where did all the money go? Where did all my time go if I haven't even built anything that's visible yet? But you and I both know that the foundation is there.

If you intend to lay the foundation for a three-story building, rest assured that it will later be impossible for you to build a ten-floor skyscraper on top of it.

If over time, you decide you want to build on these three original floors, do you really think you'll be able to return to lay a new foundation at that point in your life? Perhaps you'll be 35 or 40 years old by then. Can you really expect to go back to school to gain a better knowledge of your field? With everything else that will have happened since college—your marriage, your children, and perhaps a job or economic activity, you're left with little time on your hands.

You can ask me: "Well, Helios, what about everyone who goes back to school for a master's degree 10 or 15 years later—how did they do it?"

They already laid solid foundations years ago—what they're doing now is adding as many floors as they can add or want to add to their building, but they aren't going back and digging new foundations again.

The foundations of your training also have to do with your human relations, values, discipline, method, attitude, focus, vision, joy, enthusiasm, and professionalism—and aren't about conforming. If you can give ten, don't give eight. Prepare yourself for magnificence in life and when it arrives, you will know how to recognize it, create it, maintain it and share it.

9. Explore entrepreneurship

Do you remember that silly joke about Little Johnny confessing to the parish priest?

"Little Johnny ... who stole the alms?

"Father, I can't hear you from this side of the confessional."

"Who stole the alms!?"

"Father, I can't hear you from this side."

"Little Johnny!" (yelling this time) "Who stole the alms!?!?"

"Father, over here on this side, I swear I can't hear you. How about we change sides?

They change seats at the confessional and when the priest is on the outside . . .

Little Johnny confronts him:

"Father, who got my unmarried auntie pregnant?"

"Gee, you're right, Little Johnny. You really can't hear anything from this side, at all."

While it's true that world economies, especially those of emerging countries, need new companies in order to grow, it's also true that not all people have the right profile to become entrepreneurs, at least not successful ones.

But remember: "The best way to predict the future is to create it." And of course the best way to get a job is to invent it. If each graduate was given the task of formally creating their own job and perhaps others, our country would release 600,000 jobs every year and we would be singing a different tune.

It's worth mentioning that if you really have the ability to troubleshoot and solve problems for your potential employer and collect a salary in return, you should also have the ability to solve the problems your employer's clients have and sell them those solutions.

In 80% of the cases, you will earn much more in the short term working on your own.

About 80% of the jobs a country generates are through small and medium-sized companies. If this sounds interesting to you, find out more by visiting the Ministry of Economy webpage for your country, where you will find a wealth of support, including funds *to start getting started.*

Although I'm first an advovate of self-employment, and then of the creation and growth of more companies; I don't intend to use this chapter to convince you that you should launch a company and make your decisions about it.

What I do want to make clear is that an entrepreneur and businessperson are two different things; the first is synonymous with an initiator; the second, with an employer.

Whether you envision your life in ten years as the owner of your own business, as a self-employed person, or as a manager, director, or senior public official—stated in no uncertain terms, whether you are trying to work for a corporation or be the owner of your own, I must suggest that you venture into an entrepreneurial or business experience.

I don't care too much whether you start a business that has nothing to do with what you're studying; although you would obviously have better chances of success in an area that you're already proficient in; what matters to me is that you do it—that you simply do it.

The marbles look more fragile when they are yours, and "you can hear better on this side." Nowhere else will you have the experience, or rather the experiences, that the exercise of starting a business on your own has in store for you—you will not find them anywhere else.

Whether your business thrives or not, it will give you a down-to-earth knowledge that—let's be clear—will make a difference in your professional life.

Consider this option as a kind of "warm-up" before starting to compete, something like a period of time to prepare your muscles for open competition. You don't necessarily have to make your first business an international venture, but the self-confidence that you will gain when applying your knowledge to a business, growing it, and marketing it will be invaluable.

When all is said and done, a company's objective is to generate profits, or concrete results in the case of nonprofit organizations. Anyone who has survived the practical experience of having created and developed a business out of nothing, who can put an entrepreneurial project on their resume, who is an initiator, will have an extraordinary advantage because these accomplishments will signal to your future employers what type of person you are, and let them know that you have enthusiasm, commitment, persistence and ability to pursue your goals. And, by the way, if the business in question survives and generates an income later on, that never hurts.

10. Go for it . . . you're well prepared to run this race and give it your best!

Running a marathon, and especially training with my dad, inadvertently became our life insurance without us even realizing it. Thanks to our muscles and bone strength, we have stayed healthy in recent years. We have a high level of concentration, our lives are full of energy, and we rarely get sick. Thanks to my dad's disciplined running practice, the respiratory and cardiovascular capacity he had built up helped him survive a heart attack. I feel inspired and energetic when I'm with my children. Racing has kept me away from bed habits; it has helped me respect people more on an individual level and led me to contemplate nature. Certainly some friends have left me; the life of a lonely athlete often has moments of ingratitude. But this is my life.

You've studied 3 years of preschool—one of them in English—6 years of primary school, 2 of middle school, another 4 of high school, plus another 4 or 5 earning your undergraduate and maybe two more in graduate school.

That means you've been preparing for more than 20 years! You have faced difficult situations, dealt with arrogant teachers, with peers who want to bring you down, and with financial difficulties, sleepless nights and pressure. Sure, like everyone else, you've lived through good times and bad, but you've also been acquiring training and experiences for 20 years. Whether consciously or unconsciously, rest assured that your mind has accumulated the necessary knowledge and skills. Don't get discouraged!

Sure you can see yourself reflected in the mirror of a soccer metaphor, and I'm no die-hard fan, but it's a good example. Before a World Cup match, when a team that's preparing to win is interviewed at the airport, the usually say: We're going for the World Cup!

In turn, another team prepares to advance to the quarterfinals, and what they tell the media is: *we're just trying to advance.* How far will each national team get?

The reality that you create every day for yourself—even the reality you are already living today—depends 10% on the things that happen to you in life, and 90% on how you react to the things that are happening to you in life.

So get out there and offer your solutions to the world. Don't just look for a job; get out there and grow—build your future; don't look for any old gig, get out there and make your life an extraordinary experience, not just a matter of survival.

Come to understand and appreciate the advantages you have over thousands of people who simply never had the opportunity to access the professional training that you have today. Search inside yourself for the best you have to offer and project it outward; rest assured that when you adjust and focus your mental attitude, your training and preparation will flow smoothly, and you will surprise yourself.

> *The best way to train for a marathon is to seek out adversity. Running at an altitude of 13,000 feet, at 35 degrees Fahrenheit, in the rain, on a road under a blazing sun, in the mountains, or on the beach, are undoubtedly the best tools for your muscle memory. This isn't magic; your body simply begins to get used to the pain and grows strong. The best way to train for a marathon is to face your fears, your own monsters. The day you discover what you are capable of overcoming, you will also know yourself.*

11. Never stop training for the race

Of course as a derivative of the analogy of your career after the "race," I couldn't end this chapter of objective recommendations without reminding you that an ideal physical condition is first won, then maintained. The fact that you prepare to run the marathon and then run it, does not guarantee that, three years later, you'll still be in the physical condition to continue running. Honing and updating both your academic skills and your social skills should be a small part of your daily training.

"A muscle atrophies if not used," and knowledge that is not applied and shared is no longer knowledge. The best example of this is that when you stop practicing your English or your whatever foreign language you know, it only takes a few months of inactivity for you to lose confidence, fluency and vocabulary.

So, promise yourself to read a list of no less than six books a year related to your professional activity, and another six related to developing social skills. Attend as many symposiums, conferences, or conventions as you can. Never forget that maintaining your physical health and conditioning is much easier than getting it back again.

Of course, you have access to all the tools that I'll post sooner or later: on social media, on my blog, my webpage and on social networks or send out in an email. They are yours to use freely and at no cost; I give them to you, with my love and affection.

If you want to take your personal fitness to the next level, we've developed an app to help you train and develop your skills. If this really interests you, send me an email and I will gladly arrange a half scholarship or some preferential arrangement for you. I'll let you know that you will still have to qualify for it and that the initial minimum requirement is to have completely read this material and to pass an online evaluation regarding the information presented here; look for it at: www.heliosherreraconsultores.com.

"I will never do that again."
Felipe in NYC, 1993.

The worse moment a runner has when running a marathon is

an invisible barrier that we call "the wall." It's a supernatural phenomenon that puts you to the test when you've done approximately 20 miles of your route. You only have about 5 miles left to the finish line, but your body feels destroyed. Nearly 2 and a half hours running, a little over 2.5 quarts of sweat spilled, the sun stronger than ever, your body weaker than at any other moment. Fears and insecurities enter, "the devil," my friend Rogelio used to say. You start to question yourself repeatedly: "what am I doing here?" "Why did I start this race?" "Is it worth the effort?" "Whose legs are these that I no longer feel?" Crossing the wall is crossing any adversity that arises in your life.

Chapter TWELVE

If you find that this is difficult . . .

If despite giving the best you have to offer you find that reality is difficult, then change it. Life works according to universal laws. Perhaps one of the most powerful, or at least the most reliable, is that of cause and effect. We receive exactly what we offer; this is how it works—our actions generate the reactions of life. If the life you're living isn't completely satisfactory or doesn't satisfy you, modify your current reality by changing what you offer to life.

Offer them something different, not just the same thing packaged in a different way. Don't just exchange your usual excuses for other excuses, but replace them with concrete actions that allow you to change what you're receiving from life.

The universe is governed by laws based on plans for abundance; you should keep in mind that there is enough for everyone, there is enough of everything for everyone—even more than enough, so that some can hoard and others waste what they're given; life is like an enormous buffet table. The God you believe has invited you to life and has seated you at a table with the most delicious foods and delicacies imaginable. It's up to you whether you go and help yourself to whatever you want or let this feast go to waste on the tray.

Let me end with an example . . . Imagine how many whales there are in the ocean; give me a number, a round one; in the whole world, how many seem about the right number to you?

On occasion during my seminars, the audience yells a 10,000-population estimate at me! The internet suggests that some 100,000 specimens remain! Some sites claim there are only 600,000 of these creatures left, all species considered; but would you believe me if I told you there are only a few thousand left? On the other hand, we know that each of these animals, to keep themselves fed, gobbles up approximately a ton and a half of fish every day.

This means that if there were only 1,000 whales in the world, the ocean would have to produce around 3,086,472 pounds of fish every day just to feed them. But if the internet data is correct and there are 600,000 whales who need to eat nearly two billion pounds daily, that is, 840,000 tons per day; 25 million tons a month and 300 million tons of fish a year, just to feed the whales!

Now do you really believe that the universe operates on a model of scarcity and shortage?

The solution lies in you and me, and in what we do with our lives that improves our health and brings in abundance, happiness, family harmony, and all the good things in life.

You will notice that most of the pages in this book are now in your left hand, and so we are approaching our modest farewell. Before concluding, I want to send you big congratulations for having come this far. You should know that the statistics say that in Mexico the average reader reads fewer than two books per year per person, and that only one out of every eight books that are purchased ever get read in their entirety.

If you are reading this, you should really congratulate yourself on your discipline, commitment, and hard work! I'm not sure how long it took you to read this. I don't know where you read it, but perhaps, from time to time, I even went into the bathroom with you—although not the shower, I hope. I know that if it's been going well, you may have read me in the tub.

When I was your age, I liked to imagine the faces of authors whose books had impacted me as a young adult. I wondered what they did and how they did it, I liked to challenge them mentally and contradict them, and I would have loved to question them and check whether or not they were consistent in what they said and did, what they wrote and what their lives were really like. Today this is as simple as finding them on the web, which will always lead you to something more or less recent about authors and their books. So if you're curious, visit me on the web.

There are times when this Spanish proverb holds true: that "Another man's food will make your son good." Sometimes we are more open to hearing something from an outsider than when we hear the same things from people who love us, because we are more likely to listen with more objectivity to a stranger and to make his words our own.

When I crossed the finish line of my fifth marathon in New York on November 2, 2008. I weighed about nine pounds less than I had the night before. I felt bigger, braver, and freer than ever, even though I barely had the strength to lift my hands, take a step, or hold back my tears. I was alive.

Chapter THIRTEEN

Your career should nurture you, not the other way around

I would love to end by reminding you that you were not born to be an engineer, graduate, teacher, or doctor. Your life is much, much bigger than that. The profession you decide to spend your life pursuing will be merely a vehicle that allows you to advance towards personal growth, but it must never be the very objective of your existence.

Your professional career will surely be the mainstay of your day-to-day life, a large part of your time in this world will be spent doing things that are related to what you studied; at least, in the successful scenario that you decided to study something that really allows you to dedicate yourself daily to solve problems of your liking. Your professional activity will allow you to experience and enjoy extraordinary scenarios and possibilities, but in the end, I repeat, this will only be the vehicle that allows you to get there; you are the pilot.

Your identity cannot depend on a title or the lack of it. When you introduce yourself, don't get hung up on: "I graduated from . . . ," or

"I'm an engineer or a doctor." You are, above all else, a human being. You are an extraordinary entity that is part of a larger and more absolute whole—a human being who is here to enjoy the adventure of life itself, with all its ups and downs, but a human being all the same. Don't give becoming an engineer, a graduate college graduate, or doctor any more importance than that—I'm not saying that achieving a degree doesn't have importance, too, and sometimes really is—I just ask you never to put any more emphasis on it than it deserves.

I assure you that there are things much more important than simply "being."

It's more important to be a daughter or son, to be a spouse, and what can I even say about becoming a mother or father? Going even a little further, none of the above will be of much use to you if it doesn't allow you to be happy.

On the road ahead, dear companion or reader, a bright and peaceful sky is about to open up before you, an ocean ready to be navigated according to your directions. You are in possession of the miracle of life and it is life itself that is waiting outside for you to conquer it, to seduce it and enjoy it.

You have an extraordinary opportunity to make what you will of your life; you can literally make it an oyster or turn it into an extraordinary pearl of an adventure! In the end, despite what you may think, no one will care too much what you actually do with it. If you don't do anything with it yourself, surely no one else will.

You are the one who must live with yourself 24 hours a day for the rest of your life.

You, of course, are the one who will do or stop doing things, and of course, you're also the one who will reap the consequences for better or for worse.

I'm sure that some of the ideas and data that you will read here will shake your world. It is also likely that other details will offend some of you and that others of you may take it as a wake-up call. Perhaps some of the information will lead you to reflect on things. Hopefully, God willing, some of the ideas here will also serve as your call to action. I want your professional career to match your training. Rest assured that life is so fair that you will receive exactly what you deserve. And if you allow me, I wish you happiness and that you accomplish all that you possibly can. And may God bless you.

Thank you for your time,

Helios Herrera

ABOUT THE AUTHOR

Helios Herrera

Helios Herrera is one Latin America's most well-known Human Development, Productivity, Motivation, and Business Transformation consultants.

He draws on a 22-year career, on having spoken at more than 1,500 conferences and seminars, and given presentations to a cumulative audience of approximately 2 million satisfied participants in 12 Spanish-speaking countries and for more than 250 corporations and businesses.

He's an expert in integration processes, cohesion, connecting values, teamwork, and creating a business culture.

He is author of four books and creator of four spoken-word recordings, and contributes to several radio and television programs.

Every month he edits and shares the electronic bulletin *4 minutes to grow* through an email newsletter, along with other articles and thoughts in audio or video format, which you can ask to have sent to your inbox free of charge.

Visit our website: www.hhconsultores.com You can also enjoy our videos on YouTube: "Helios Herrera."

If you're looking for strategies to develop your work team through high-impact activities based on actual experience, want to schedule a face-to-face conference, or simply want to talk with him, please contact Helios directly at helios@hhconsultores.com

ABOUT THE CO-AUTHOR

Felipe Hernandez Tovar

Felipe Hernandez Tovar is the director of Greenbox Design, a design and creative advertising production company; though he also really enjoys his work as a writer and conceptual artist.

In 1993, at the age of 22, he ran his first marathon and discovered the hidden secrets between long-distance running and life's wisdom.

He has since participated in more than 300 races in Mexico City, Buenos Aires, and New York City, where he completed his fifth full-length marathon in 2008. Felipe runs with his dad, virtually, every time he puts on a pair of tennis shoes.

He is father to Emilio and Natalia, two future runners on their own careers path, who are his sources of inspiration.

Felipe is a friend of Helios Herrera and a staff member at HH Consultores.

To reach him, send an email to greenbox_fht@hotmail.com to receive his electronic publications for free.

Your Career after the Race

The keynote address

Based on Helios Herrera's latest book

Don't miss your opportunity to reach your goals. Go further and share your race at "Your Career after the Race" with others in the student community. Visit the academic coordination and ask for the calendar of upcoming presentations by Helios Herrera for your place of learning. They know the terms and conditions.

Visit:

www.despuesdelacarrera.com and join our running community on the web after your race.

Documentary review

Video Paradigms

Discovering the Future, 1989, Joel Barker's show: This video talks about the future, change, and to the opportunities that paradigm shifts can bring. And most importantly, it introduces people who have a pioneering spirit; a special group of people who convert the new paradigms from merely a concept into a practical reality.

ManpowerGroup. Connecting Latin American talent to the job market.

2008 http://www.manpower.com.mx/sala/documents/ei/La%20Integracion%20 al%20 Mercado%20Laboral%20del%20Talento%20Latinoamericano.pdf

The video describes the elevation of Latin America's labor markets and includes very useful information about our market position and through trend analysis provided by thousands of employers working in different fields and specialties and with different sized companies.